keeping a journal
you love

SHEILA BENDER

keeping a journal
you love

WALKING STICK PRESS
CINCINNATI, OHIO
http://www.writersdigest.com

Visit our Web site at http://www.writersdigest.com for information on more resources for writers.

To receive a free weekly e-mail newsletter delivering tips and updates about writing and about Writer's Digest products, register directly at our Web site at http://www.writersdigest.com.

05   04   03   02   01   5   4   3   2   1

Library of Congress Cataloging-in-Publication Data

Bender, Sheila
  Keeping a journal you love / by Sheila Bender.
    p.   cm.
  Includes bibliographical references (p.) and index.
  ISBN 1-58297-068-8 (alk. paper)
    1. Diaries—Authorship. I. Title.

PN4390.B45   2001
808'.06692—dc21   2001017613
                                                              CIP

Edited by Meg Leder
Designed by Sandy Conopeotis Kent
Cover photography by © Kamil Vojnar/Photonica
Production coordinated by Emily Gross
Author photo by Pranesh Cadman

This book is dedicated to everyone who has helped me learn to value solitude, to understand its presence and to glory in its special light.

ACKNOWLEDGMENTS

I would like to thank my editors, Jack Heffron and Meg Leder, for focusing on journal keeping and offering me the opportunity to write on the topic again in the hopes of enticing more people into keeping journals for insight and for pleasure.

I also wish to thank the authors whose journal entries and comments on journaling appear in this book. They are as generous as they are helpful. We have made every effort to maintain the personal style of each journal keeper in regards to idiosyncratic punctuation, word choice and abbreviations.

Finally, I want to thank my daughter, Emily Bender, and her husband, Vijay Menon, for their patience and understanding concerning a mother-of-the-bride, who was down to the wire on making the deadline for this book as their wedding approached. May they rejoice in their marriage always!

ABOUT THE AUTHOR

 The author of five books on writing, Sheila Bender is currently a contributing editor to *Writer's Digest Magazine*. She teaches poetry and personal essay writing, as well as how to keep a writer's journal, at the University of Arizona Extended University. She is adjunct faculty at Loyola Marymount University in Los Angeles and teaches at the annual summer Colorado Mountain Writer's Workshop. To find out more, visit her Web site at www.SheilaBender.com.

TABLE OF CONTENTS

PART ONE

dances with daffodils

CHAPTER ONE

learning to keep a journal you love

If you have picked up this book, you are probably very well intentioned about beginning a journal or learning new ways to keep yourself interested in keeping a journal. With writing teachers, classroom teachers, celebrities, psychologists and even doctors espousing the intellectual, emotional, psychological, spiritual and health benefits of journaling, it seems that you should love keeping a journal.

However, although your heart is in the right place, if you haven't kept a journal or been happy keeping one in the past, you may feel adrift as you enter an open-ended sea of daily or weekly writing sessions. If you already keep a journal, you may crave more inspiration, like a sturdy ship that needs to refuel. In addition, whether you have done much writing or not, and even if you love writing, you might not like your own writing enough to keep at it. Whether you are new at journal keeping or have been doing some already, you may also have trouble enjoying the time it takes to keep one. You may feel guilty stealing time to write or even thinking of doing so when other tasks need your time. If you also write for a living, you may feel that since you are not necessarily going to refine and publish everything you write, you are wasting time journaling. Whatever your journaling situation may be, you have come to the right book. Being in the presence of fifteen professional writers through some of their journal entries and their commentary about keeping a journal both inspires and informs. Ideas gleaned from professionals from and about their journals will help you get serious and go about getting the most you can from keeping a journal. The entries themselves will show you how professional writers use journaling to stay open and human despite sorrow, rejection, confusion and ambition. You will read entries and discussions that foster contemplation, observation and engagement with the world and cultural opportunities as a way of enhancing life. In addition, when you read the entries of professional writers and their words about their journaling processes, you will learn how journaling helps them stay productive. Through them, you will experience how important and possible journaling is. In addition, when you use the strategies I've developed based on the journal entries, you will find help getting meaningful words onto the page, often about topics you had no idea you could write about.

Before we get to those entries and exercises though, I want to coach you in the three elements of journal keeping, as I know them. If you come to the exercises versed in these elements, you will have a big jump start in keeping a journal you love. These elements are: (1) a compulsion to get things down the way you experience them (or at least the ability to see the benefit of such a compulsion), (2) a desire to enjoy some solitude (or the vision to understand that you can learn the art of enjoying it), and (3) an understanding about how to incorporate the craft of creative writing into your entry writing. Right now you probably have more ease with one of these elements than the others. My intention is to help you build all three elements into your journaling life by discussing solitude, answering questions about journaling and instructing you in the craft of writing. Then, in the following chapters, I'll offer helpful words of well-known American authors. After each writer's sample, I'll propose many journal-writing ideas inspired by that contributing author's entry or entries. With the combination of my instruction, your reading of the author entries and the exercises I propose, you'll get going in journal keeping with a strong start and sustain your momentum over time. When you harness a developed talent for entering solitude to a developed understanding of writing strategies and skills, you begin to nurture a healthy compulsion to get things down. This is because you make the time to do it, and by using writing skills, clear the space to do it. Finally, you may want to join with others who love to journal, and in chapter nine, I have included ideas for doing so.

the compulsion to get things down

When he was seventeen years old, the American writer, lecturer and transcendentalist Ralph Waldo Emerson began keeping a journal from which he would ultimately pull ideas for his essays and poems. When he was twenty-four, he wrote this entry while he was in Charleston, South Carolina:

> There is a pleasure in the thought that the particular tone of my mind at this moment may be new in the universe; that the emotions of this hour may be peculiar and unexampled in the whole eternity of moral being.

This is the attitude that best aids the journal keeper who, through the making of regular entries, is on a hunt for the best articulation of the way she experiences her world and the events around her. Even if you are too humble to believe that what you have to say or what journaling helps you find to say is a "particular tone of your mind" that "may be new in the universe," you must act as if you believe this when you journal. Writers, whether of journals or plays, novels, poetry and fiction, believe they have something original to evoke about experience. They also believe they must do this for their mental and emotional well being.

Just as Scheherazade learned to tell compelling stories night after night because she believed her life depended upon it, believing in a possibly unique "tone of mind," as Emerson did, will help you find the very best articulations of which you are capable. Then your inner life will come to depend upon the driving force of your new belief.

the enjoyment of solitude

First and foremost, keeping a journal is an act of honoring solitude. According to my *American Heritage Dictionary*, 2nd college edition, solitude is something very different than isolation, which can be of whole groups. Solitude implies one person and is about being alone, but not in dejection and desolation. Instead, solitude is a state of being that fosters contemplation about what is at the bottom of our minds and in our hearts. It is a state in which a wide variety of feelings come to inform us about our lives and those of others we are concerned about. I think of the Sonoran desert as I write this. Instead of being a dry, arid place inhospitable to plants and animals, it is in fact a dry, arid place that fosters the presence of particularly wonderful animals and plants. It is a desert full of birdsong from quail, cactus wrens, mourning doves and woodpeckers. There are frogs, lizards, snakes, scorpions and many varieties of cacti, bushes, shrubs and trees. Some years the wildflowers bloom profusely. Solitude is like visiting this particular desert—when you set out to journal and you take time for the solitude in which to journal, you may fear you are going to a desolate place. However, once you take the time and put pen to paper, using the exercises in this book as a guide, you will find your solitude is rich with sounds and images, a world of splendor grown from your own impressions.

Solitude is hard to come by in a busy world. Many of us are not alone or away from distracting stimulation long enough, or we are not in the mind-set to explore our thoughts and feelings often enough. In addition, we too often shy away from solitude because we're not sure what we'll find there. Luckily, in beginning a journal, even with short entries, you start to honor solitude because the writing takes you there. You soon find yourself exploring not only your thoughts and feelings, but carving out a bigger and bigger oasis of solitude to do this. Talking from inside yourself to yourself on paper is a way of making sure your life builds and includes solitude. You begin to experience how enjoying minutes and even some hours of solitude on a regular basis makes you sturdier and more effective in dealing with your life.

You may think that talking with a friend or loved one helps you do the same work of getting out observations and thoughts as does keeping a journal, but there are leaps of association you can take in writing that you can't take in conversation without losing your listener. There are also thoughts you have when no one is around that writing allows you to explore. Writing lets you start out with seeming non sequiturs and then find out what you are thinking, whereas conversation usually has to have a purpose and an understood starting place. Last, but not at all least, in conversation you field the responses of the people you are talking with, and this impacts and alters what you say. In journal keeping, you do not have to read anyone's expression and tone of voice or address expressions of worry and misunderstanding unless you want to!

In solitude you can explore, take in, give out, breathe

freely, get to know yourself apart from others and apart from images you hold of yourself. It is a powerful tool for increasing self-awareness, finding one's center and greeting the world from a wonderful, wise place.

Whether you sit down to write about your day by recording thoughts that have surfaced, descriptions of people and conversations that came your way or landscapes you took in, you are taking time to be with yourself. Alone with yourself and your writing, you will find out more about what you appreciate in your life and about the effects your inner and outer worlds have upon your life and thinking. Even if all you do is log in facts about mood changes or food intake, you are still taking the opportunity to sit alone contemplating something you have done or thought. More information about your thinking and feeling will arrive if you listen for it. So journaling in a blank book or a plain notebook (which works just as well) ensures that you will reach the important, wonderful place of solitude.

dances with daffodils

In college, I studied the English poet William Wordsworth, who lived from 1770 to 1850. I think that was the first moment I "heard" a writer telling me how important being alone with my own thoughts was for living well. Wordsworth's accessible poem "I Wandered Lonely as a Cloud" speaks volumes about the value of taking time for your inner life apart from others. I believe his poem is a whole treatise on the value of solitude in making us sturdy. For

Wordsworth, wandering lonely as a cloud is not desolate—
it is a happy loneliness. Clouds share the sky with birds and
have the other clouds as neighbors, and they can "see" all
that goes on below and above. However, each cloud is distinct, separate, undispersed and in and of itself—like you!
Here is Wordsworth's poem:

I Wandered Lonely as a Cloud

I wandered lonely as a cloud
That floats on high o'er vales and hills,
When all at once I saw a crowd,
A host, of golden daffodils;
Beside the lake, beneath the trees,
Fluttering and dancing in the breeze.

Continuous as the stars that shine
And twinkle on the Milky Way,
They stretched in never-ending line
Along the margin of a bay:
Ten thousand saw I at a glance,
Tossing their heads in sprightly dance.

The waves beside them danced; but they
Outdid the sparkling waves in glee;
A poet could not but be gay,
In such a jocund company;
I gazed—and gazed—but little thought
What wealth the show to me had brought:

For oft, when on my couch I lie
In vacant or in pensive mood,
They flash upon that inward eye
Which is the bliss of solitude;
And then my heart with pleasure fills,
And dances with the daffodils.

You might want to write Wordsworth's "I Wandered Lonely as a Cloud" inside the front cover of your journal as a reminder of the value of solitude, both the solitude in which the world springs forward into your senses and the solitude in which you recollect that happening. *Keeping a Journal You Love* is filled with discussions and strategies that help you perform both the taking in and the recollecting of your "daffodil fields," both the pleasing kind like Wordsworth's with all the flowers dancing in the breeze and the less pleasing kind with shriveling blossoms or still and heavy air. Even if the entries you create contain sadness, having relived events to put the sadness on the page brings relief, and in that way, the joy Wordsworth is talking of.

the FAQs

Before I introduce the first writing strategies to increase or refresh your skill with the craft, I would like to answer some questions seasoned journalists continue to think about and many people ask when they begin journaling.

How is a journal different than a diary?

Some people say there is a difference between the two, but I believe the terms are now used synonymously, with journal being the favored term. The word "journal" comes from the same root as the words "journey" and "day." A journey was originally described as how far you could travel in a day, and so a journal was originally a record of a day or of the thoughts of a day. It now seems to me the word "journal" is more identified with the journey one takes by writing, day after day, in the hopes of finding better understanding and a fuller world.

What kind of notebook or blank book is good to use for my journal keeping?

Again, an inexpensive notebook works just as well as a more expensive hardbound blank book. Some people want hardbound books because they are sturdy; others want spiral notebooks because the binding doesn't get in the way as you are writing. Three-ring spiral notebooks are a happy compromise if you only want to carry paper with you and then collect your entries in one place that looks more permanent. Some people think putting a little money into the purchase makes them more serious about keeping the journal; others feel soft-covered notebooks are less intimidating.

Whatever kind of journal you choose (and you can always change what kind you are using when you finish with one of them), try to develop a fondness for it. Some things that help you do this are: (1) giving the journal a title such as "So Far This Year" or "Patient Listener" or "This Is What I Think" or some other title that speaks to you, and (2) write or paste into the journal or onto its covers quotes, poems, fortune cookies and horoscopes with special meaning for you. The journal is a place of inspiration, and keeping words that matter to you near your own words helps you find that your own words matter more and more.

Can I use a computer instead of a notebook?

Using pen and paper is the most common way that people begin journaling. A pen and notebook can go practically anywhere with the journal keeper, further guaranteeing that she will take the time to get outside of time for a few minutes' solitude a day. However, laptops are portable, and you may prefer using a keyboard to handwriting. In addition, many people like having an audience to keep them writing. E-mailing ongoing journal entries to a fellow journal keeper can help guarantee that you'll take the time to journal. If you are sharing entries, you will, of course, have the recipient in mind as you journal, and this might shape your entries. This is most helpful if you find a recipient to whom you feel you can address whatever you wish. Such an audience may call out the performer in you and keep you writing longer and more frequently. Obviously, U.S. mail works for this kind of exchange, just more slowly.

How often should I write in my journal?

I think once a day as many days of your life as you can. Some people find one or two days a week to journal when they have time to sit at a cafe or go to a park and write. Other people clear some journal-keeping time each day, before work, during lunch, after dinner or just before bed. Experiment by writing at different times and in different places as often as you can, and see what schedule and places work best for you. Some of us write better from a nook or cranny at home; others write best out in the world where we can be by ourselves. I do best in my car, parked where I can see water. I can get to my favorite kind of place between teaching assignments, early in the day or at sunset. I try for a variation here because I believe the information and thoughts I access in myself differ during different times of the day.

How can I keep my journal private and safe from others' eyes?

There is no foolproof way, of course, except perhaps to get a safe and store the journal in it. Most people find a private place to keep the journal in their room, or they reach an understanding with those around them that this notebook is private. If you feel uncomfortable because someone may read what you have written, perhaps you can find a place to keep the journal where no one will have access to it—a locked drawer at work or in your study, or your car trunk or glove compartment, for instance. But don't make the hiding place so difficult to get to that you are parted from your journal at times when you would be using it to gain solitude through writing. I think the more we journal, the more comfortable we get with our journals and the more accepting we get of ourselves. Then although we don't want others to read what we've written without our permission, we are less frightened about them doing so and less suspicious that they will.

What am I supposed to write in my journal? Are there topics I shouldn't write about? Are there some I would be remiss in not writing about?

In journal keeping there are no topics that must be covered and none that are forbidden. My favorite journaling techniques use a prompt or exercise that helps me get very quickly to memories I hadn't thought I'd be writing about or poignant thoughts I didn't know I'd figure out how to articulate. Rarely do I know ahead of time what I will be writing about. I let the journal-writing exercises direct my writing. However, if you have something you want to explore in writing, exercises can also help make your exploration more meaningful and more deeply lived.

Learning to use specifics, details and images along with some other writing craft strategies helps you write well. Doing the exercises later in this chapter will help you gain the confidence to use specifics in your writing. Incorporating the particulars of what you see, hear, taste, touch and smell allows you to enjoy the writing process and mine yourself for more and more images that you can write down each time you journal. Using the techniques I describe in the following journal-keeping strategies will give you a good start, a start in which you are intrigued with your own thoughts and experiences, and by your reexperiencing of the world as you write. Using these exercises, you will find that in the state of solitude, you have dipped deep into the well of living, surfacing from the well with refreshed feelings and experience.

practicing the writing craft

Following are seven exercises for developing creative writing skills. Do all seven exercises in your journal, and you will find yourself remembering to use your new writing skills in doing the later journal entries suggested in this book, entries based on strategies of professional writers. As you continue to journal, you can always return to making entries using one or more of these seven exercises whenever you need to jump-start your journal writing or remember how to make your writing image-oriented and specific.

You can even make a point of devoting one week each season of the year to using these seven strategies. At the end of the year, take a look at your four weeks of exercises and see how your writing has grown, how you have been able to apply the writing strategies to ever more topics, issues and interests.

So here we go! Devote this first week of keeping a journal you love to having fun doing these exercises now.

the seven sisters: journaling exercises to help you begin

First and foremost, writing is a re-creation of experience—experience we have in the world and experience we've had within ourselves. Experience is lived through the five senses. It is what we see, hear, smell, taste and touch that add up to the impressions from which we form our attitudes, take actions and create dreams. The seven sisters exercises are aimed at helping you quickly get to the kind of writing that offers this experience. Even though you are only writing for yourself in your journal, if your writing does not include details and images that appeal to the five senses, you will not be immersed in experience when you are writing. Without the necessary immersion, you will become disinterested in your own efforts because your words will seem shallow and dull. In addition, you will short-circuit your ability to mine your experience if you stay with intangible and editorial words. If you say "beautiful" and "wretched," for instance, you are telling yourself how you think you feel toward whatever you are writing about. Imagine you think a philodendron in your living room is beautiful. If you say, "The leaves on the philodendron in my living room had variegations that reminded me of tributaries on the maps I loved to read when I was in grade school," you are setting up experience that cannot be had by labeling the leaves "beautiful." If you describe yourself as feeling wretched the morning after a breakup, imagine how much more experience you can evoke by being specific with words and details that appeal to as many senses as possible. You can say, "I woke up twisted in my bedsheets which imprisoned me. My sadness was a warden I expected to keep me in lockdown. How could I face the day ahead, even by myself, with a headache as big as Texas across my skull?"

1. writing what you see

You may come to the page thinking that you cannot possibly get down accurately and interestingly in words what you observe through your eyes. Don't be intimidated. By adhering to the following ideas, with a little practice, you will be writing fluently and with momentum, allowing your words to describe a world, inner and outer, seen through your eyes. When you report what you see literally, you are actually also reporting your attitudes toward what you see. You are showing, instead of telling. You are trusting your images to offer the feelings as well as the reportage. In this way, writing what you literally see leads to the writing of your attitudes about what you see. With something on the page to actually see, not just something referred to as having been seen, your writing becomes richer. This richness will help you keep writing in a way that interests you. In other words, instead of saying something is exciting, show that it is. Writing "The birds were exciting that day" is not as rich in experience or emotion as writing "As the bright red cardinal visited my bird feeder, I watched two goldfinches sit awhile in the Canadian thistle, eager for a turn themselves."

a. Look at an object in the room or place you inhabit

right now. Describe what this object—say, a desk—looks like without relying on adjectives. Instead of saying "the rectangular wooden desk," say, "The desk is made of pine, with ten boards about six feet in length joined side by side to make the width of a canoe's belly." Now that the word "canoe" has come up, it is easy to leap to an association like "and lucky days, writing at this desk, I feel myself paddle without a ripple among lily pads and marsh grasses, capturing the tadpoles and minnows of my thoughts even as they dive under the water or hide behind the tall grasses under the wide leaves." Look for images to "leap" from your words. Then take the leap.

b. Practice with the writing strategies of comparing images to refresh experience using similes (when you use a "like" or an "as") and metaphors (when you say one thing is another thing). Utilize sight comparisons to widen your observations and bring in fresh experience. All writers need to have facility with this kind of comparative thinking. It enlivens your writing and your view of the world, and it thereby keeps you happier and more intrigued with your writing. You can practice this simply by saying one thing looks *like* another:

A mirror looks like a lake.

A cornflake in a bowl of milk looks like a dolphin swimming in the ocean.

A shoe with its lace untied looks like a toaster with its electric cord unplugged.

Now try metaphors. Say one thing is another thing:

> I sit at my desk, a marionette with no one holding the strings.

> The thirty student papers on poetry in my briefcase are a thick sandwich.

> Dressed up in the front seat of my husband's convertible without a scarf on my head, I see my hair in the visor mirror, madly waving fronds at the top of a stately palm tree.

Write lists of your own that are like these two as a way of exercising your simile/metaphor-making mind using the sense of sight.

2. writing what you hear

Sound is all around us, yet we overlook putting it into our writing. We say something is loud or soft, quiet or noisy, but we don't try to sound that way in our writing. Here is one exercise to help you get your words to imitate the sounds in the experiences you are writing about. Then we'll do the metaphor/simile exercise again, but this time with sound images.

a. Think of a noisy place—your street on garbage collection day, a room full of third-graders when the teacher isn't there, the kitchen when you are chopping onions and running water in the sink. Then describe the sounds of this place, using words that are as quiet, as staccato, as smooth or as loud as what you are describing. Read my example and then try your hand at doing this.

On garbage collection days, the disposal company my husband calls Loud and Early slams and smashes its way into our sleep. We hear the sounds of garbage cans colliding with the thick rusty truck, then scraping and clattering across the asphalt and cement of street and curb. When we hear the garbage truck grind the dregs of our existence to a pulp, we slide our feet to the floor. A police helicopter overhead hurls its hello, shaking the walls and shattering any memory of our dreams.

When you write to get your experience on the page, remember to incorporate the sounds of the world you are experiencing as you write or have experienced and are remembering.

b. Now do the metaphor/simile exercise using sounds. Here are some examples to read before you write your own comparisons:

The sound of a train going by in the distance is the sigh of a ghost.

The ocean crashing against the shore sounds like the blood in my veins heard through a stethoscope.

The tones and tunes of cell phones ringing in the

purses and pockets of Los Angeles restaurant diners at lunchtime make even the most sedate and refined establishments sound like carnivals.

You might want to go outside if you are writing inside or inside if you are writing outside. Listen for some new sounds that you can use to write metaphors or similes.

3. writing what you smell

Often times we smell something and a flood of memories comes back—marinara sauce or pot roast cooking on the stove may bring us back to our childhood home or our grandmother's house. The smell of pies baking in the oven may remind us of a bakery we worked in during high school. The smell of janitors' floor-cleaning substances might remind us of our dorm cafeteria in college. The smell of tobacco or coffee on someone's breath or the smell of fresh mown grass or coconut oil on sunbathers takes us back years to other times and places we've experienced. In writing, we must never overlook our sense of smell.

   a. Write down three smells you are aware of right now—e.g., your own perfume, something cooking, burning oil from a car going by, water from a hose, charcoal in the grill, baby powder on a toddler after bath time, the new plastic smell of casings on electronic components. Think of what the smell reminds you of. Write about your memory, starting out with: "I sit here and smell _____ . This smell brings me back to_____ . That's when I _____ ." Keep writing for ten or fifteen minutes remembering to include more smells from that time remembered. If you'd like, read my example as a warm-up:

I sit here and smell the pages and binding glue on my new book. This smell brings me back to flour paste and papier-mâché days in my Brownie troop and grade school. That's when I made maracas by coating burned out light bulbs with strips of newsprint soaked in nontoxic paste made of flour and water. Strip by strip we covered the bulbs, layer upon layer of newsprint, until none of the glass we'd started with showed through. I think we must have waited for layers to dry before we added more wet newsprint over them, smell of a wet dog, I think. Somehow our teachers knew when it was time for us to declare the musical instruments done. Somehow the glass got smashed without our damaging the papier-mâché casing we'd painstakingly created. Then we painted our instruments bright colors. They began to smell like new patent leather shoes. I think we must have used them, broken glass both hitting and missing the beat, like the sound of my multivitamins in a jar on the breakfast table when I lift it to serve out tablets.

b. You probably noticed the smell metaphors in the writing (wet newsprint, smell of a wet dog) as well as the sound metaphors (broken glass inside the hardened papier-mâché sounding like vitamin tablets in a jar). Take some time to write some metaphors and similes that connect smells in a way that refreshes (makes you reexperience) experience:

The smell of clothes fresh from a dryer is like the smell of bread baking.

The smell of the charcoal grill after the fire has died down is like my girlfriend's clothes after the fire in her apartment.

Smell of jasmine flowers as I walk by is the smell of my grandmother's dress as I clung to the folds.

4. writing what you taste

Unless you are a food reviewer, you are probably more apt in your writing to say something tastes bitter, sweet, salty or bland rather than more fully describe the tastes of things. Here is an exercise to get you concentrating on the sense of taste:

a. Put something edible in your mouth. Keep it there awhile without chewing it. What does it taste like so far? Then bite into it and write what it tastes like a little more dispersed in your mouth. Now chew it and describe the taste. Now swallow it and describe the taste left in your mouth. Use similes and metaphors if they help. Here is an example to read:

SOYBEAN

I roll you around with my tongue and you are wet
from the rinsing I gave you, and you are cold from
the refrigerator so you taste a little like a glass of water.
I bite into you and I taste the smallest flavor of salt,
as if there were a single tear on my tongue. When I
chew you up good, I am surprised by the taste of
something just a bit like the smell in the stagnant
puddle a gardener's hose leaves at the foot of my apartment's driveway. It is so vague, though, that it is not
at all unpleasant. I swallow, and you leave the taste
of grass I remember from when, as a child, I sucked
on green blades in summer.

b. Again, write more metaphors and similes in a list, this
time for more practice using the sense of taste. Sometimes
we forget to include impressions that come to us through
our sense of taste, although we often say that something
we want is so close we can taste it when we mean we are
enthusiastic about whatever it is. In using metaphors, we
can ascribe tastes to things that we don't really put in our
mouths—it is a way of describing and evoking an internal
reaction to something that grounds us in the experience.
Here are some examples of metaphors and similes that rely
on the sense of taste. After you read them, write a list of
your own that utilizes the sense of taste.

My anger is cayenne pepper in my mouth.

When I make my college students laugh, it's as if I have seltzer bubbles in my mouth.

My children's hopes and dreams taste like vanilla and honey in gently warmed milk.

5. *writing what you touch*

In writing, using the sense of touch is probably second only to using the sense of sight. Our skin comes up against the elements and soaks in information all the time. Our fingers go out to greet the world by holding objects, stroking pets and loved ones, and shaking hands with strangers. We touch the fabrics of anything we sit on, open, close, deliver or use.

a. You can do the following exercise to make yourself aware of your sense of touch and how to incorporate it into your writing: Think of something you are very familiar with touching—an article of clothing, soapy dishwater, a pot scrubber, your cat, a garden rake, the driver's wheel of your car. Write about the feel of it in detail, using similes and metaphors if that helps. Here is an example from my writing:

> I plunge my hands into the soapy dishwater in the white Rubbermaid tub in my sink. It is warm as the morning coffee I sip and swallow. It slides over my skin like lotion. Now it feels buoyant around my hands like risen dough. I keep my hands in the soapy water before I pull the first dish out because I like

feeling like a goldfish must in a bowl swimming in sunlight from a nearby window.

I am surprised by how much I like part of the act of washing dishes! Perhaps if I chose something else, I would be surprised by dislike:

When I put my hands inside my pantyhose, gathering it so I can slip my toe inside, my fingers snag the fiber like rough little emery boards. I pull the hose up along my ankle, calf and thigh, feel its pressure grip my skin. At first, I like the way the hose seems to hold my skin together like the bread of an orange under the peel. But when my two hose-covered legs brush against each other, I feel each one begin to itch. I want to take the hose off then as if it were a bandage I didn't need. Later when it sags at my ankles, I feel the downward pull, a sensation like I have in my stomach when the elevator goes up.

Now you take a turn describing something you touch by using metaphors and similes to evoke the very sensations you feel. Try to choose something you don't know how you feel about so you can see that the very images you use and the comparisons you make start to show your feelings.

b. Make another list of metaphors and similes using images that express touch. Try filling these in and then if you want to do more, make up your own beginnings to find endings for:

Your skin next to mine feels like _____ .

When I touch my feet I feel the _____ off
a _____ .

The overripe canteloupe feels like _____
between my fingers.

When I hold a cup of coffee in my hands, the china
is hot as _____ .

6. writing using anaphora

In addition to using sensory imagery and turbocharging
your writing with metaphor and simile, counting on certain
types of repetition can help you write well using details
from your experience. The literary term for one type of
repetition is "anaphora," and it means repeating the same
word or phrase at the beginning of a series of sentences.
With this kind of repetition, you gain momentum in your
writing and your writing gains power because you have a
comfortable structure within which to place sensory details
and specifics. In the Declaration of Independence, for instance, Thomas Jefferson used anaphora to explicate the
offenses of King George III against the colonists:

He has refused his Assent to Laws . . .

He has forbidden his Governors to pass Laws . . .

He has refused to pass other Laws . . .

He has called together legislative bodies at places unusual . . .

He has dissolved Representative Houses repeatedly . . .

He has refused for a long time . . .

He has obstructed the Administration of Justice . . .

He has made Judges dependent on his Will alone . . .

He has erected a multitude of New Offices, and sent hither . . .

He has kept among us, in times of peace, Standing Armies . . .

He has affected to render the Military independent . . .

The poet Walt Whitman is famous for relying on anaphora. You'll see the device used in almost any section of his famous book-length poem *Leaves of Grass*. Here are a few lines to serve as an example:

And I know I am deathless,

I know this orbit of mine cannot be swept by a carpenter's compass,

I know I shall not pass like a child's curlicue cut with a burnt stick at night.

I know I am august . . .

Try your hand at acquiring writing momentum and power by doing the following exercises based on using anaphora. You will see how repeating phrases helps you think of more to say and helps your writing stay cohesive in a way you might not have been able to achieve without using the repetition.

a. Write your own Declaration of Independence from someone, some activity or some subject area, starting each line with "Because you have . . ." and finishing it with particular details like Jefferson did. When you have generated a long list, announce that you are declaring yourself independent, and switch to writing about what you will do with your independence: "Now that I am free, I will . . ." and finish each sentence in your list with details about what you will now do. You can choose things to declare your independence from such as a dishwasher, a car, an obsession with getting the love of someone or a task you have set yourself. For instance, you can declare your independence from the idea of being a perfect employee, daughter, mother or wife. You can declare your independence from wanting to read mysteries or watch TV or play computer games. You get the idea. No matter what your topic, as you do this exercise, you will gain experience with the momentum of anaphora.

b. This is a story about . . .

For this exercise, think of an event you would like to write about—a holiday at your house or someone else's house, an annual trip to the state fair, a vacation to the Bahamas or Hawaii or Europe, a meeting at work, etc.

Don't say what the event is, but write about it in separate lines or paragraphs that each begin with "This is a story about. . . ." Fill in details after "about." Remember the lessons of the first six sister exercises as you write using all your senses.

Here is an example:

This is a story about saguaro cactus, barrel cactus, cholla and prickly pear in the dry heat. This is a story about their white blossoms and their yellow blossoms. This is a story about long-branched ocotillo with red flames at their tips, the green-branched pale verde looking as if it were drawn from one crayon. This is a story about cactus ribs long as doors drying in years of sun, of real live mistletoe seemingly tossed like woven scarves in the branches of mesquite trees. This is a story about mesquite trees, fragrant after rain relieves the desert's dry heat. This is a story about the taste of sun in my mouth like warm bread, the feel of it on my skin like cashmere. This is a story about cottonwoods, whose seeds blow like fairies over the small stream from snowmelt far away. This is a story about cactus wrens and woodpeckers, about quail and roadrunners moving fast across the asphalt from one patch of desert to the next. This is a story about the mourning dove's cooing and a little rabbit on its side, dead in a pool of blood because it could not hop fast enough and was hit by a car. This is a story about a place without the ocean but not without the ocean humans unleash over the landscape, capable of blotting out what we cherish most.

Try your hand at using the "This is a story about" repetition to practice gaining momentum in writing.

c. Once I wanted to be . . .

Imagine yourself or remember yourself thinking about the circumstances you wanted for yourself during your life. Think big and think small—you may have wanted to be an airline stewardess as well as the planter of California poppies along roadsides; you may have wanted to be the owner of a certain house, couch or car, the wearer of a certain ring or the mother of a certain number of children. And you may have wanted to be talented enough to sing in *Madame Butterfly* or dance the lead in *Swan Lake*. Be specific in each line or paragraph that begins, "Once I wanted to be." Range in your thoughts and writing through your material world, fantasy world, natural world, occupational world and world of talent. When you have written many, many lines beginning "Once I wanted to be," change the repeated sentence opener to "But now I am" and again range through the different areas of your life. Here is an example:

Once I wanted to be a rabbi and develop the consciousness of an entire congregation through sermons that moved them to tears and to laughter and to quiet thoughts.

Once I wanted to be best friends with Susan Sarandon, keeping her company as she cared for her kids and made movies.

Once I wanted to be an elephant for a day so I could see about curling my trunk and stretching it out, about kneeling on my knees with so much weight and squealing in a very loud voice.

Once I wanted to be a skilled carpenter so I could build anything I needed for myself.

But now I am someone who hires others to hang shelves and assemble unassembled furniture.

But now I am sitting alone in my loft in a city I have hardly lived in thinking of visiting the ocean.

But now I am petting three cats.

And now I am doing my e-mail, smiling at the number of others waiting for my response, my information, my greetings and my love.

And here are two more writing exercise ideas to help you incorporate the use of anaphora:
d. Because my time here is short . . .
In the book *Tuesdays With Morrie,* a dying man grows ever more instructive in his lessons to us about our connections to the world and to others. He is deeply aware of his life because he is not going to live too much longer. This kind of awareness can come to us when we write if we

imagine ourselves with limited time to appreciate and enjoy. Do this exercise thinking about a place that you are: in a meeting, on vacation, in a classroom, paying bills, cooking dinner, visiting with a friend. See what happens when you describe yourself in that situation by dividing up your actions and thoughts and introducing each of them with the words "Because my time here is short. . . ."

e. If I were rich (or kind, sincere, happy, loving, open-minded, an inhabitant of a different place) . . .

Most of us have dreams and ideas of what we'd be like and do if we had unlimited resources or were able to move to a different part of the country. You can write about these ideas whether or not you are aware of all of them by using the repetition of "If I were." Whether you are using personal traits you know you have or ones you wish to have, the repeated "if" helps you explore and write more fully. By isolating the trait and fully imagining yourself with it, you will find yourself creating experience on the page.

7. writing using metonymy

I am taken with the way common phrases in our language rely on our using just the right detail to give a lot of information about a person or location. We say "our head" when we mean "our thoughts." We say someone doesn't have "a leg to stand on" when we mean that they can't justify their actions. When we use body terms to convey abstract or intangible feelings and ideas, we are using a strategy called "metonymy." This strategy heightens our ability to experience what is on the page. For instance, in "One Art," a famous poem by Elizabeth Bishop, the speaker is coming to grips with grief over the departure of a loved one. Bishop writes, "—Even losing you (the joking voice, a gesture / I love) . . ." Here two details stand in for the whole person and bring us closer to the speaker and her subject. This is definitely what we hope for in journaling!

Using metonymy in your writing can help you describe people and places you know by extracting one or two gestures or attributes to stand in for the whole person or place and express the way you experience that person or place. For instance:

> On my father: When I was young, you were a god with thunder in the clearing of your throat.

> On my house on the Olympic Peninsula: I miss the garden, magenta buddleia and blue-flowered cotoneaster.

> On my job at Loyola Marymount University: Hard to feel academic in a classroom full of tank tops and sundresses.

Now you choose some subjects, and select one or two details that will tell the whole story of how you experience them.

In practicing the seven sisters writing exercises, you will have already begun taking the time to build solitude into your life. You will have learned techniques for giving voice to who you are and how you experience life. Now, when you turn to the following chapters containing the entries of professional writers and their discussions of why and how they journal, you will notice their use of the same writing skills you have practiced. As you listen to them share the ways in which journal keeping helps them honor as well as use their solitude and compulsions to get things down, you will feel the power of each journal keeper's re-creation of lived experience on the page.

As you use the coming exercises I've based on what the professional writers are doing in their journals, you will have an easier time filling your own journal with the sound of your voice. And it won't be a stifled, this-is-in-writing-so-I-have-to-sound-important voice. You will have created a treasure of connection to your true self. When you read your journal over, you will recognize the sound of this voice and the joyous feeling of having belted out your own song. Who knows—perhaps the tone of mind you represent will, in fact, be new in the universe, and perhaps you'll look forward to joining the larger journaling community!

PART TWO

stolen pages

CHAPTER THREE

day-tripping

You have probably read or heard about the historic journals of boat captains, overland merchants and military
men. You have probably also come across the published
journals of prisoners, exiles, servants and pioneers. Although these journals may be famous now for the information they include, the authors' main motivation in keeping
them was most likely to keep track of themselves and the
events they were encountering. In the case of prisoners,
exiles, servants and pioneers, journals kept them connected
to their lives and motivated them to go on despite harsh
circumstances. In the case of the others, journaling helped
them stay aware of and connected to the details of sometimes overwhelming daily events. As a reader, you may have
been grateful to these men and women who fluently and
painstakingly put their worlds on the page, day by day,
week by week and month by month.

When you travel or work away from home for extended
amounts of time, you may be moved to keep a trip diary as
a way of making sure you will never forget where you were
and what it meant to you. Journaling about new settings,
people and sites can be invigorating, keeping you from laps-

ing into the same old thoughts and words. On the other hand, maintaining a trip journal is daunting—you wonder how you'll be able to write in a way that captures the importance of the trip and the intricacies of what you experience. Most likely, there are weeks and months between the trips you deem important enough to journal about.

To address both the probable lull and possible intimidation I am talking about, I suggest that you bring the attitude and experiences of the traveler to your journal keeping every day. In this chapter I will share travel journal entries by three contemporary American writers along with commentary they have written about themselves as journal keepers on those occasions. After each author's entries and commentary on those entries, I will suggest exercises you can do in your journal that are guaranteed to keep you in a traveling frame of mind, whether you are away from home or at home. You will be inspired to capture your travelin' self, one day's journey at a time.

Kathleen Alcalá's journaling example

Novelist and short fiction writer Kathleen Alcalá kept a special trip journal when she went to Mexico to research the second novel in a trilogy she was writing. She stated:

In 1990 when my son was three months old, I completed my first book, *Mrs. Vargas and the Dead Naturalist*, and entered the manuscript in the King County Publications Project in hopes of receiving funding for its publication. I was ready to turn what little attention I had left over to a new novel, which I would call *Spirits of the Ordinary*. My uncle who was eighty-four was sick and dying. My cousin had three children I'd never seen. *Spirits of the Ordinary* would take place in Saltillo, which is five hundred miles east of Chihuahua, the city where I had spent part of every year growing up and where my relatives still lived. The cities were similar enough in ambience that I could research as I visited my family whom I had a terrible urge to see.

Once in Chihuahua, Alcalá discovered something very precious to her research. Here are several journal entries leading up to and including the discovery:

> *24 de Mayo, 1990*
> *Chih, Chih, Mex.*
> *Chih. Is much the same to me, though big and dirty and noisy. Priscilla says they have built machinaderas (industrial towns) so people have come from all over, from the south, to work in them. Impoverished-looking settlements, raw cement bricks with no trees, are springing up everywhere. There is not enough water for them. The land is stricken. I don't remember it ever so dry.*
>
> *My aunt and uncle have moved. It's only a block from Calle de la Llave, a street name I loved. They live on Paso Leal, and Priscilla next door.*
>
> *It looks beautiful walking in—a spacious tiled passageway full of plants 1 story high (the plants). It leads past a living room and dining on the right, a patio, a stairway on the left.*

At the back, the kitchen on the right, a room with my uncle, now bedridden, on the left. He lies in a hospital bed, blind, unable to talk, but he responded to my talk and touch, and loved touching Ben's soft skin. He is 84. The rest of the room holds a big bed with a colorful spread, cozy furniture. This is clearly where my aunt spends her time. The upstairs is unused, the patio full of weeds. The back of the house peters out to a vacant lot.

26 de Mayo
Francisco was born on a hacienda near Saltillo of working people. 84 means he was born in 1906. Mexico had changed little from the 1500s to 1910, so he was born into the old class system, poor. He had to work since he was a boy, so it was important to him to have a big house. Wayne and I walked around upstairs—1 huge room after another, many with their own baths. There is no water connected upstairs. There is a big studio/library which I will visit tomorrow. On a drawing board is a pastel study of an owl. He had been painting owls before he lost his eyesight. Ruth and Prissy each have one. Julieta says I can take any painting I want, but I don't want to take any off the wall, although I love them. Some of the still lifes of fruits and vegetables are so vivid and so much a part of my permanent childhood memory that when I see them, I almost don't see them.

The land is dry. El llanos en llanas. People yearn for rain.

Jan Feb Mar Apr May Jun Jul Aug Sept Oct Nov Dec
      Dry   Wet
      Easter   Christmas

27 de Mayo
Francisco's Library
Books all dusty and mixed up. Books on Mex history, esp.
Northern Mexico; famous artists' biographies, bios of famous
musicians and composers (classical); books on homeopathic and
natural medicine; books on Christianity; world encyclopedias;
many Spanish dictionaries; profiles of historic Mexican figures;
popular novels by Mex. Writers, books from Spain; translations
of books by Am. Authors—Pearl S. Buck, Hemingway, Dosto-
yevsky, Steinbeck. "Yo, Robot," por Isaac Asimov; a Spanish/
English dictionary printed in the late 1700's. Books by rela-
tives, including Manuel Acuña and José Garcia Rodriguez.
Books about Sor Juana; Gabriela Mistral; important women
in world history.

Many of the books in F's library had titles like "Hidden
Pages," or "Stolen Pages," or the "Hidden Mexico." The tables
upstairs have bookends—a small, ornate globe—a colorful paint-
ing of birds on cuero, popular for the last 20 years or so—
beautiful pottery on the bookcases. Priceless. Candy and wrappers
left by Priscilla's children. Photos and portraits of F all over.
Many of the books are inscribed by the authors to Prof. Cepeda.

Julieta played some really old gospel records for Wayne while
I was upstairs. It sounded like Perry Como sings hymns or
something. Scratched and well used. She also knows all about
Julio Iglesias. Ruth went to Las Cruces to hear him.

Books
Medicamentĕs Indígenes, *por Geronimo Pompa, 1972.*
Relatos misterio y realismo, *por José García Rodriguez,*
1947.

Los Mexicanos Pintados Por Si Mismos, *orig. 1855, reprinted 1946.*

Cuentos del Mexico Antiguo, *por Artemio de Valle Arizpe, 1953.*

Antología de Poetas y Escrituras Coahuilenses, *1926.*

Los judíos bajo la inquisicíon en hispanoamérica, *Boleslao Lewin, 1960.*

Libro de Chilam Balam de Chumayel.

Manuel Acuña, *por Francisco Castillo Najera, 1950.*

Obras, *por Manuel Acuña (poesías, teatro, articulos y cartas), 1965.*

Poesías de Manuel Acuña, *segunda edicion, 1968.*

Obras completas de Concha Espina, *1944.*

Ms. Alcalá wrote the following in contemplation about her trip journal:

I needed something to hold in my hands in the far north, in the rainy winter of Seattle and be able to say, "No, I didn't imagine it. It really is like that in Mexico. People really *do* sing in the streets and advertise cooked food for sale and the sky is bluer and the mangos sweeter. People *do* live in the moment instead of waiting for something better to come along." I needed to see my own handwriting telling me, "This is what Mexico is really like. I did not just imagine it." Of course, that's impossible, since we re-imagine everything our senses tell us just as soon as it enters our brains. But still, I thought I would try.

The novel I was working on, *Spirits of the Ordinary*, takes place in the late 1800s in a city another five hundred miles east of

Chihuahua. It is where my aunt's and mother's ancestors were from, and it is not much known or written about. It is also difficult to get to from Seattle, Washington, and it would have been impossible to visit both Chihuahua and Saltillo in one trip. I opted for my living relatives, especially since my uncle was not expected to live much longer. Even though my son was less than a year old, I felt it was important for them to meet Ben, and I suppose there was sort of a "baptism of dust" involved in bringing Ben to Mexico, the home of his ancestors.

On the other hand, life in northern Mexico has not changed all that much. Chihuahua is known for its Federalist (mid-1800s) architecture and its revolutionary history, and while the city is not the same, I felt that a lot of the ambiance would be duplicated in both Saltillo and Chihuahua. Both cities are commercial centers, rather than tourist destinations. Both cities have been in existence for several hundred years, and both have been heavily influenced by their proximity to the United States. Most interesting to me is the mixing of cultures—Indigenous, Spanish and European—that has been going on all this time and the particularly fierce and independent outlook it has fostered.

My uncle Francisco Cepeda Cruz was both unusual and typical of the citizens of Northern Mexico. Born to peasants on a hacienda, he became, at the age of twenty-one, director of a prestigious private school in Chihuahua, a post he held for fifty years. Upon his retirement, he received a medal from the president of Mexico for his outstanding service to education. A self-made and largely self-educated Renaissance man, he painted in oils, sang, composed poetry and read prodigiously. A devout

Protestant, he was generous with his friends and silent about his enemies. I had found him both formidable and wonderful as a child.

Francisco's library had been a source of wonder since my childhood. It probably helped to shape my bookish nature as an adult, and I was eager to spend time in it, since I knew that it had invaluable source materials for my own writing. At the same time, I was interested in the space of the library, the idea of the library. I had come to realize, walking around Chihuahua, that architectural space in Mexico reflects the public and private lives of people. Plazas, fountains and grand buildings are set aside for communal use. Houses present a forbidding facade to the street and are turned inward, built around an open courtyard where the family can move freely, and the division between interior and exterior is loosely defined. Catholic homes often have private shrines inside, and the idea of a personal library seemed even more private and interior to me. Perhaps, in our Protestant subculture, a love of learning had replaced faith in the institution of the Catholic Church.

It had not exactly been off-limits to us as children, but we were not supposed to bother Franscisco if he was working in his combination library/studio. With five children plus their friends and cousins, this was probably a matter of survival. Still, it retained an air of the tantalizingly forbidden, which I was to use for a library in my novel:

Esaías walked along the wooden portico to a small door and knocked. This was his father's study, and only the old man had a key to this door. After a moment, the door swung slowly inward, leaving Esaías straining to see into the gloom of the interior before stooping to enter the doorway. His father was already reseated behind his massive desk, as though he had willed the door to open of its own volition.

The small, sallow-skinned man sat regarding his son with large unblinking eyes like some nocturnal creature.

Esaías always felt awkward in this study, large and clumsy among the fragile books and stacks of tissue-thin papers that would crumble to dust in a good gust of wind.

Here lay his father's treasure. Here were his books, the books accumulated one at a time, sometimes a few pages at a time, smuggled in saddle bags surrounding preserved foods, or wrapping a trinket from overseas. It had taken thirteen generations to compile this library, thirteen generations since all things Jewish, all signs of learning and Hebraic study had been burned by the townspeople of Saltillo, since Esaías' forebears had gained the lives of their wives and children by changing their names and agreeing to be rebaptized into the Holy Roman Catholic Church.

Esaías stood in this dark, crowded room, hemmed in by precariously balanced stacks of books, half-empty inkwells, broken quills and glass vials of mysterious chemicals. He stood too tall, his shoulders hunched under the weight of thirteen generations, under the name he bore, pinned against the six-inch thick door at his back by his father's unblinking gaze. Esaías had no love of books, of tradition, or of enclosed places. He had come to tell his father good-bye.

My grandfather, Miguel Narro . . . kept journals from his mid-teens until his death in 1955. A minister who traveled and lived all over the Southwest, his journals also functioned as his sermon notes and business records, but on occasion, he included long descriptions of people and places otherwise lost. They include some of his dreams and his notes from teaching himself how to read Hebrew. I now have these journals, and they seem to radiate a magic of their own when I open the brittle covers and see his careful handwriting. They are his legacy to me, the only living writer in the family.

There is an air about life in Mexico that keeps it from ever seeming quite of this world. Perhaps it is true in all of Latin America, where the past and present run together, where reality is determined as much by faith as by scientific evidence. No amount of journal keeping can pin down this quicksilver quality, which is just as well. In any case, I came across a paragraph that seemed to sum this up, and I hope it applies not only to the books in Franscisco's library, but to my writing as well:

Foreword to "La Mandrágora," a story in the *Antologia de la Literatura Fantastica Espanola*, 1969, ed. Jose Luis Guarner:

La presente historia, aunque verídica, no puede leerse a la claridad del sol. Te lo advierto, lector, no vayas alla-marte a engaño: enciende una luz, pero no eléctrica, ni de gas corriente, ni siquiera de petróleo, sino uno de esos simpáticos velones típicos, de tan graciosa traza, que apenas alumbran, dejando en sombra la mayor parte del aposento. O, mejor aún, no enciendas nada; salta al jardin, y cerca del estanque, donde las magnolias derranam efluvios embriagadores y la luna rieles argentinos, oye el cuento de la mandrágora y del barón de Helynagy.

In English:

This story, although truthful, cannot be read in the clear light of the sun. I advise you, reader, don't try to deceive yourself: turn on a light, but not electric, not of gas, nor of petrol; perhaps one of those quaint lanterns, so graceful-looking, that barely cast any light, leaving in shadow a major part of the room (lodging). Or better yet, don't light any-thing; go outside to the garden, and near the pond, where the magnolias pour out their intoxicating fumes and the moon makes silver tracks, hear the story of the mandrake and the Baron of Helynagy.

| *your turn*

Taking your lead from Ms. Alcalá, use some of your journaling time to capture the mystery in a day spent traveling or a day spent at home or work. We take a day trip every day of our lives when we view our time here on earth as full of surprises.

1. Write about a building you spent time in on a particu-lar day. Name the street it is on and what the building is called if it has a name. Write about its textures, size, colors and function. Describe what surrounds it. You could use the "This is a story about" strategy in chapter two to help you gain momentum in finding the details you need.

2. Choose one person from the building you were in and describe this person fully. Use sensory impressions so you are

involving yourself fully in the experience of being aware of the person. It can be someone you know or someone you encountered for the first time. You may use dialogue as a sound impression.

3. Choose one place in the building you are describing—a room, a mezzanine, a lobby, a garden, a garage. Write about this place like you are trying to memorize it. After you have shown what is in the space, what it sounds like and what the smells are and possibly the taste in your mouth, write about what is most surprising in this location. Even if it is a small detail, include it and discuss the surprise. In Alcalá's entry on her uncle's library, she notes the discovery of books with titles like *Hidden Pages* or *Stolen Pages* or *Hidden Mexico*. Although Alcalá didn't know it then, her discovery was important. She later found out something extraordinary, as you see in the novel excerpt—her uncle was one of Mexico's hidden Jews.

Al Young's journaling example

Novelist, screenwriter, poet and feature writer Al Young details the following about his journal keeping:

My early teens coincided with the early 1950s, a time when I was devouring books from the Detroit Public Library and buying with money earned from shining shoes and janitoring downtown at the Sidney Hill Health Club—cheap, keepable paperbacks. My reading included such thrillers as William Saroyan's *The Twin Adventures*, Albert Camus's *American Journals* and Knopf's two-volume edition of *The Journals of André Gide*. The Saroyan book especially intrigued me. It combined the text of a novel, *The Adventures of Wesley Jackson*, with a charmingly chatty journal of equal length that the author, an American G.I. stationed in London during 1944, had kept while writing it. Characteristically, Saroyan had knocked out both manuscripts in a mere thirty days.

From such books, I gradually got the idea that keeping a diary or journal gave you the freedom to write (or not write) anything you damn well pleased. That you were also free to make entries any time you wished gave me a curious little rush. I reacted quite differently, however, to Saroyan's seemingly informal "record keeping" than I did to Gide's or Albert Camus's, or to most of the other literary journals I had begun to study and comb. When I read even the childhood diaries of those larger-than-life literary Frenchmen, I could tell right off that their meticulous, delicately-phrased entries represented something else again.

To whom had the ten-year-old Gide or the twelve-year-old Camus been directing their largely intellectual reflections, observations, assessments and asides? Decades later I would conclude that these men-of-letters, even as children, tender prodigies, knew all about critical literary audiences and formal journal-keeping, to say nothing of posterity. Saroyan, on the other hand, gave every appearance of writing largely for himself, for the sheer fun and hell of it.

Quickly I lost interest in what a journal or a diary was *supposed* to be; instead I became absorbed with discovering or fashioning doors and windows that opened right up to me when I playfully hurled myself or tiptoed into my own unsupervised journals. After all, with myself as the targeted, pre-sold, fully subscribed audience for those pages, how could I possibly lose? Mostly I wanted to get down something about the crazy turns and bends my days and nights had taken, something I imagined I'd find fascinating, gripping or, at the very least, *useful* at some distant time—moods, thoughts, mysteries, illusions, passions, changes, the works. Discovery, excitement, the unchartable high of monkeying around with time and traveling through it—these were rewarding facets of journal-keeping that stunned and stimulated me then fully as much as they do right now.

The following is a sample from Young's journal made November 5, 1986. It captures a day's discovery and excitement as he aimed to:

It's funny how time works these days; every moment is accountable. I suppose it was always so, yet now that I nakedly have no one to blame for things that don't get done, I look at the passing of so-called time differently; it's all blossoming out of me and my on-goingness. For example, this weekend was spent in Los Angeles, where I continued to hang out with Gary Larson, the cartoonist I'm writing the profile of for the New York Times *magazine. Larson was giving a talk at UCLA, so I thought this might provide an excellent opportunity for me to look at him from another angle: in a setting outside the privacy of his home in Seattle, which is where the previous weekend was spent. Monte Kay has invited me to stay with him and his wife Roberta for a night before moving on to the Sunset Marquis Hotel for the following night. At the last minute, though, his plans have changed; he and his wife can go to dinner with me, but the futon I slept on last time is now in his daughter Susie's room and Roberta's son is visiting. Anyway, the guest room scene has shifted and, besides, they're just back from a Caribbean jazz cruise and so they're still catching their breath.*

So what do I do? I pull an Al Young; that is, I land at Burbank Airport, rent a Chevy Nova, drive around looking for the first motel that looms in view, and end up at a place called the Bali Hai out in Sepulveda in Van Nuys. It's $30 a night, but it also turns out to be a low *dive; a rendezvous joint for hookers and their johns and their pimps and male prostitutes and probably dope traffic too. While I'm getting ready to take an afternoon nap after check-in, I hear a soft knocking at my door but I'm too weary to answer. Later that night the Kays treated me to a yummy Mexican dinner at the Border Grill (where chile relleno with beans and rice and salad tallied in at $14.50 and where the waiters and waitresses all looked like Martin Mull or Farah Fawcett) on yupscale Melrose Avenue. You talk about fern bars and trendiness! So after I've collapsed for the night back at the Bali Hai, I'm awakened at 3:30 in the a.m. by what sounds like a party going on in the parking lot beneath my window. Pulling back the curtain, I peep out and see a couple of the women chatting good-naturedly with their men while engines are idling and people are patting one another on the butt and—well, there you have it. The next morning right after meditation, I check out, drive down to the Santa Monica Pier, gather a batch of screenwriting class assignments from the car and go sit on the beach in the sun to do papers.*

It always feels like Nathanael West's Day of the Locust *whenever I'm in L.A. Even the people walking past or jogging past my bench on the pier seem like extras, like either they'd been famous long ago or are straining to get discovered somehow. It's nerve-wracking. But there was a rather remarkable thing that happened after I packed up and left Santa Monica for Hollywood. No sooner have I driven the couple of miles up the Coast Highway to Sunset than my attention is drawn to a hitchhiker right there at the intersection with her thumb out, looking every bit like one of the students I teach at Uncle Charlie's Summer Camp (as the kids call UC Santa Cruz). At great peril to my health and the rented car, I pull over and she hurries in. She's 22, blonde, impeccably dressed, very pretty and British; Scotch, really, but quite the Anglophile. Her destination's Beverly Hills. Our talk while I forged through murderous, smoggy midday traffic up sunset goes something like this:*

"I know it probably seems odd," she says, "for someone like me to be hitchhiking, but I'm broke and don't have a car and this is the only way I can get around."

"Where you from?"

"Scotland, but I know my accent's English."

"Been in California long?"

"Two years."

"Like it?"

"I really do. My parents think they're going to lose me to Southern California. I would like to enroll at Santa Monica College next year and study business, brokerage in particular. And you, what do you do?"

"I'm a writer."

"Oh, really! What sort of thing do you write?"

"Novels, poetry, articles. I'm down here now doing a piece on a cartoonist, Gary Larson, who does 'The Far Side.'"

"How exciting! Yes, I'm familiar with that strip. I just finished a book myself."

"About what?"

"About my walk across America. It took 151 days. My name's Ffyona Campbell, and my walk across the States was sponsored by the Campbell Soup Company—there's no relation, however."

"Did you make the Guinness Book of World Records?*"*

"Yes," she says, clearly delighted. "I'll be in the next edition. Writing is difficult, isn't it?"

"Do you have a publisher yet?"

"Not in America, but in the U.K., yes."

On it goes in this vein, with Ffyona advising me about which lane I should be in and how I might want to snake around this car or that limousine. It's Indian summer with a vengeance; hot, actually in the 80's and still November, can you believe it? Palm trees are swaying and people seem to be generally in elevated spirits; at least drivers aren't honking or cussing at each other much.

At the mention of Seduction By Light, *Ffyona practically squeals with excitement. "What's it about?" she asks.*

"Well, it's actually set right here in Beverly Hills and Santa Monica. She's a domestic who's also psychic and has an illegitimate son by a previous employer. She senses that she isn't going to live long, so she wants the boy and his father to get to know one another, and—"

"Oooh," she says, "it sounds a bit like White Banner!*"*

"Like, what?" I say, the title suddenly drowned to me in the unexpected tartness of her English tones and traffic noise.

"White Banner," she repeats slowly. "It was published around 1942, and it's also about a domestic who's psychic and who's had a son out of wedlock by a previous employer."

"You're kidding!"

"No, not at all."

"Where is it set?"

My heart is beating, even though I know the book can't possibly be anything like mine. All the same, I've made up my shocked mind to track the thing down.

"I'm looking for a job," Ffyona tells me after I've recovered.

"Anything in particular?"

"About the only kind of work an alien like myself without papers is qualified to do: work as a domestic."

"Can't you be an English nanny?"

"No, and fortunately that sort of thing has gone a bit out of style here. I'm glad because I couldn't do it anyway. I find the idea distasteful."

And so I let her off someplace around Sunset and Rexford—which isn't far from where Poitier lives, I recall—in Beverly Hills, and I drive to the Sunset Marquis, where rooms let for $150 a night, check in, plunk down my Visa, and disappear into the world of doing school papers, going down for a Jacuzzi, then spiffing up for the meeting with Larson's publisher, his syndicate publicist and Larson himself that night at UCLA. Afterwards we go out for dinner and it's already past 10:30, joined by Melanie Kirsch, sister to the publicist. And Melanie's got a book newly out about drugs that's got a lot of bread behind it; she's going on all the big TV shows like Donovan and David Letterman, and such. She turns to me in the back of the car and says, "So it looks as if I'm going to make a lot of money." Larson's coming down with the flu and can't wait to get away. I've got to teach in the morning and so I'm eager to get to bed.

By the time Vicky Houston drops me and the publisher George Parker off at the Marquis, it's almost one in the morning. I pack up, as you might've guessed, and sleep like concrete, rise at 5, shower, jam down the elevator, settle my bills, hop in the Nova, remember to get gas before I get back to the rental site, dash into a 7-11 out near the Burbank Airport for coffee, which I snap a lid onto for drinking while I finish up my papers on the plane, but it's too close to take-off time, which is 6:53 a.m., so I end up leaving the coffee at the ticket counter, make the jet by the skin of my minty teeth, land in San Jose an hour later, find my Tercel, stuff my belongings inside it, motor to Santa Cruz and on it rolls like a dream.

But imagine the chances of picking up a hitchhiker who'd read such a book as White Banner? *That's the kind of thing keeps me on my inner toes.*

In describing this entry, Young wrote:

By spring of 1986, I had been invited (as a last-minute replacement for an applicant who had cancelled) to spend three months at an artists retreat: the Pamela Djerassi Foundation, a ranch tucked away in the bucolic hills of lush Woodside, California. That was where I happened to complete that novel, which is dramatically set in and around Hollywood. The story is narrated by Mamie Franklin, a singer and sometime-actress turned Beverly Hills maid for a prominent film producer and his foreign-born wife. Mamie, a middle-aged charmer, who knows she isn't long for this world, is, as she puts it, "setting her falling-down house in order." Not the least of Mamie's concerns is Benjamin Franklin, her only child, who has just graduated from the UCLA film school and who has yet to learn that his real father is a big-time film and TV producer, a former employer and lover of Mamie's.

. . . The autumn of 1986 found me visiting Santa Monica, one of the settings I had more or less re-created for *Seduction By Light.* This was where Mamie lived. I remember sitting on the Santa Monica Pier, looking around me, imagining that I hadn't done badly in my depiction of that rebellious, enigmatic community which, because of its many municipal programs, was being called the People's Republic of Santa Monica. Driving back into Los Angeles along the Pacific Ocean, I picked up the lovely hitchhiker from Scotland . . .

Later, back at home up near San Francisco, I found the book she mentioned, *White Banner* (which I had never heard of before), although I had seen the movie made in the 1950s from one of Douglas's other novels, *Magnificent Obsession*; similarities between my maid character and his blew me away. Like everything else that has blossomed in time from seeds first planted in journals and diaries I've kept, the imponderable coincidence of having met Ffyona Campbell—a voracious reader who had also made *The Guinness Book of World Records* by walking across the United States in 151 days—continues to blow me further and further away. The ever-melting wonder of it all!

୧𝒫 | *your turn*

Here are more journal-keeping ideas, inspired by Mr. Young's entry and discussion, that will keep you observing, responding and thinking like a traveler:

1. Review your day or week for synchronicity—

coincidental events that have surprising connections. Were you thinking you needed to move and someone offered you an apartment at low rent? Were you thinking about someone you knew a long time ago and then bumped into someone else, who you then found out knew that person before you did? Were you feeling lonely and a kitten found its way to your door? On a trip, what fortunate breaks came your way just as you felt lost or defeated? Write the story of the day or the week previous to this event. Describe the state of mind you were in, where you were, what demands you had to meet, how you thought about the situation you were in. Describe the places you were during this time as well. Now describe the synchronicity you experienced. How did this change your feeling, thinking or approach to your day or your trip? When you establish an awareness of synchronicity, time takes on a new dimension, a "blossoming out" as Young calls it. Try to record synchronistic events as often as you can in your journal.

2. Pull an Al Young; that is, do something like his adventure of landing at the Burbank Airport, renting a Chevy Nova and driving around looking for the first motel that looms in view. Whether you are traveling or at work or home, you may want to do a version of this suitable for a short amount of time: At lunch, decide you are going to walk until you see three dropped coins on the sidewalk or three stray cats or ten people in gray coats or whatever you determine. Write about your journey. Describe where it took you and where you found what you were looking for. Describe the find. How has attaining your goal changed your day?

3. Think about a time you had an important engagement you had to travel to, or write about one happening now or one you wish were happening. Are you traveling by car, air, boat, bicycle or foot? What is your destination? Who else is involved? How does it all turn out?

Joan Weimer's journaling example

The following journal entry is by Joan Weimer, an English professor, editor and nonfiction writer. At the time of her entry in January 1973, she was traveling in Egypt to understand the lives of women struggling with poverty, repression, and war:

We follow the sound of bagpipes, *of all things, to see a wedding procession winding up the spiral staircase of our hotel lobby. Belly dancers in red and orange spangles and veils flounce up the stairs, castanets clicking. What are they doing at a wedding? Young men in the party invite us to come along, and upstairs we see the bride, hefty in white satin, holding a little boy on her lap. Beside her on the dais the skinny groom tries to make conversation, but she never responds or changes expression through any of what follows:*

At the other end of the room, the belly dancer—young, plump, pretty in a snappy way, dressed in red bra and brief and net midriff and skirt—bounces to the hard erotic beat of the music. She looks more like a high school cheerleader—"Let's hear it for sex!"—than either a seductress or an artist. Then she climbs up with one foot on the chair of the bride and one

foot on the groom's, gets the bride to clap a few times—and
bumps and grinds right in their faces.

    What's a belly dancer doing at a wedding in a culture that
values a woman's chastity more than her life?

In later travel journals, Ms. Weimer remarked that she
"wrote about torture in Brazil, about bombings of clinics
and day nurseries in Central America—all paid for by my
tax dollars." Her journal became "the repository" of her
outrage. Weimer noted:

When I wasn't traveling, I was too busy living my own life—as college
teacher, writer, activist, mother, wife, friend, cook and tennis
player—to record it. Then a vertebra separated from my spine. The
trauma of surgery flooded me with unfamiliar feelings and disturbing
dreams. To clear my brain, I wrote them down. Long months of
convalescence with no guarantee of full recovery gave me, for the
first time since adolescence, the leisure and the urgency to examine
my life. Who could I be if I could no longer do the things that had
always told me who I was? When I was finally able to mosey into
the woods next to my house, I wrote this:

    October 20, 1988: Radiant yellow leaves floating down
from maple trees, pine needles drifting down to carpet the
ground. The "dying" trees are just as much alive as the "ever-
greens." They have different life cycles. That's all.

    In some strange way, I'm more "alive" in this strange new
life—hibernating, horizontal, mulling things over, connecting
by long telephone lines to friends and family—than I was doing

my stimulating, pressured, gratifying work. Incredible.

My journal became a place to pursue a feeling or a dream instead of forgetting or evading it. In my journal I could say "Life stand still here." I'd never forgotten those words of Virginia Woolf's for what an artist does.

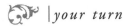 *your turn*

After reading Ms. Weimer's journal entry and her words on journaling, think about how your journal can be a repository of insight gained from keeping the traveler's keen eye for detail and seeming incongruities:

1. During a trip or on any day, sit on a balcony, terrace, park bench or by a window. Look at the people, animals and objects passing by. Record what you see at first, freewriting about the scene for five minutes. Then look up and record one more thing. Write about this for five minutes, then do it again. Reread the three freewrites. Freewrite for five minutes about what you think these three subjects shared being in the same place, seen at different times.

2. Weimer describes the bride and the groom by their expressions, actions and physical shape. The details she includes speak volumes. Choose people from your trip or day—people you are traveling or working with or those you just encounter. Use one detail about size, one about shape, one about what they are desiring and one about how they are reacting to the world or to someone or thing in it. Then write a metaphor evoking the way you experience these people similar to the way Weimer wrote that the belly dancer seemed like a cheerleader for sex.

3. Weimer tells us that on one end of the room, the bride holds a little boy on her lap, and on the other end, the belly dancer bounces to the beat of the music. Adopt this idea of at one end and on the other, or on one side and on the other, or in the morning and in the evening, or last week and this week, here and at home—any opposites of space or time will do. Write about what is in one place or time and then switch using a phrase such as "on the other side" or "in the evening," and write about what's in the other place or happening in the other time. Such a focused juxtaposition will lend a rich resonance to your observation.

Seeing yourself as one who journeys forth each day into surprising moments and scenes will help you write journal entries that portray life as you have uniquely lived it!

musings, meditations and tidbits

J ournaling can be a tool for storing tidbits of description and thought you find intriguing or mystifying, for writing meditations and for noting personal musings from your reading and attendance at lectures and exhibits. You may want to express fanciful sides of your imagination triggered by seeing people and events, or you might want to entertain quick what-ifs or dramas that go by in a flash. You might like to meditate with pen to the page, allowing yourself to make leaps of association between what you hear, see, taste, touch and smell, and what you are currently reacting to in your life. You might use a pen and paper to extend playful musings or considerations you had during your day. You might be attracted to a particular way you or someone else describes a person, place or thing. A pithy description may linger. Short exchanges of conversation make an impact. Sometimes a song lyric or a line for a poem arises in your mind, but you don't yet know the rest of the song or poem.

The three writers whose journal entries appear in this chapter are masters at recording some of these occasions. Read their journal entries and their comments about what they use their journals for. Then try your hand at the exercises I propose to help you use your journal to store and foster entertaining phrases, liquid ponderings and incisive musings.

Ron Carlson's journaling example

Fiction writer Ron Carlson numbers the entries he makes. Here is an example:

24. How it's impossible to point someone's hand at a star, the star you're talking about.
38. Getting off the phone, she always put a fire in the excuse.
55. Names: Nan Moist, Margaret Ability.

Explaining what he is up to, Carlson writes:

Who hasn't taken world notes? Who hasn't written down some comment or observation that had absolutely no use or application to the current projects, some phrase that insists on being sketched in the margins of a history notebook or the back of an envelope? What are these things? I remember as an undergraduate worrying that I wasn't fit for college because I couldn't resist all the marginalia potshots that suggested themselves during lectures. What do you do when you're acting sophomoric and you're a senior? What about later—and later and later unto now—as I am still inking odd inklings: names and coined words, what-ifs and descriptions, titles and dreams, images and connections? What I once thought was an entertaining quirk has become my clear custom, and I've learned a few things about getting some good out of it.

60. All the songs were taking their lyrics from tattoos.
61. Titles: Asides.
88. Make love the way a construction worker has an accident with a wheelbarrow of cement.

In some ways these scraps are the physical manifestation of the way my mind works, sparks flying off the wheel. They're pretty, but you couldn't cook with them. The challenge is always to find a way to utilize each of these minute inventions, line them up and make them work. Well, that's not exactly going to happen, but I continue to write and gather these strange and distracting odd bits.

99. I discover myself on the verge of the usual mistake.
110. Painting: Landscape with fortified building.
30. They discovered that the elevator in their dilapidated building acted as a bellows for the air conditioning, so they sent the child out an hour every afternoon to ride up and down.

The day I finished the first draft of my first novel, *Betrayed by F. Scott Fitzgerald*, in the summer of 1976, I cleared my table and dumped my journal onto it. My journal those years had been a large Z.C.M.I. shopping bag which by that August was full of half a bushel of little papers on which I had scribbled: envelopes, folded memos, torn slips, wedding announcements, rodeo programs and such. It made quite a pile. What I did was sit there and type them up, one item at a time, dropping them back into the bag. I'd already rescued this treasure chest from the curb where my wife had put it as garbage, which it resembled more than a little—though I hadn't inscribed any remarks on banana peels or tin cans. This transcription took me all afternoon and was just the kind of exercise that's almost refreshing after finishing a manuscript. There was little thinking involved. What remained of my journal now were about nine sheets of single-spaced items, some only a word or two, some several paragraphs and one (transcribed from the theatre program for *The Mousetrap*, a school production my wife had been in) was more than a page. Immediately, I went through this freshly typed miscellany and penciled where I thought each entry might fit into the novel. It was fun, having all these smart remarks. Like working with a committee of the alert, the off balance, the witty. I'm only smart from time to time and here were many of the times. I was able to find a home for three quarters of my observations, and I wove them into the book when I did the second draft, thickening the broth nicely.

I find that if I'm in a project, writing a story, my current observations are likely to find an immediate home. If I'm between things then my random notes go into the random file which is literally a file folder in the filing cabinet in my study. It's a first cousin of the shopping bag. Once or twice a year when I am in need of an activity that requires no thinking, I pull this folder and type it into a computer file titled "Notes," which is simply a second cousin of the shopping bag. Right now there are several hundred items in "Notes," more fabulous gems, I fear, than I will ever find proper settings for. This hasn't stopped me. I continue this irregular activity, regularly adding to my eclectic inventory. I appreciate what Dawn Powell said about journals and notebooks, their being a writer's "promissory notes." That's got it. All these things are little debts, most of which I will never pay.

204. Stark as in stark naked.

271. You can tell by the way people drive in a city how many lies have been told there.

✿ | *your turn*

I think we all would like to see in writing "the physical manifestation of the way" our minds work, "the sparks flying off the wheel." If you are not already aware of thinking in clever, entertaining description and aphorisms, of seeing both the sparks and the wheel, here are three strategies to do just that:

1. Let participles force you to be wise. Carlson notes, "Getting off the phone, she always put a fire in the excuse." "Getting off the phone" is a participle. Make a list of several participles. For example: climbing out of the car, balancing on the edge of the pool, yelling at her kids to come indoors for dinner, toasting bread in the morning. Now write finished sentences that start with the participles, and then introduce a person who "puts" something literal like fire into what he or she is doing:

Climbing out of the car, she always felt she was putting a bear's paw into a circus ring.

Balancing on the edge of the pool, the young girl in her bikini put a little MTV into her performance.

Yelling at her kids to come indoors for dinner, she put enough hysteria in her voice to crackle the length of the power lines.

Toasting bread in the morning, she put her day's hopes in with the bread like a dusting of confectioner's sugar.

2. "They discovered that the elevator in their dilapidated building acted as a bellows for the air conditioning, so they sent the child out an hour every afternoon to ride up and down." This is an entertaining scenario! What might you discover and what might you put into action to utilize your discovery? Here is an example:

Because I discovered that my cats' scratching altered the upholstery on my couches, I let them do a patch every day and then I came with darning needles and embroidery paraphernalia and wove a beautiful array of colors into the tatters. Now people all over the world order my handmade, cat-scratched fabrics. I have just sent one of my fabrics to a count in Belgium. He. . .

Let yourself consider crazy discoveries and what happens as a consequence of your discovering them!
3. "You can tell by the way people drive in a city how many lies have been told there." What an interesting philosophical (with the tone of the empirical) statement. Become

a philosopher in your journal. What can you tell from what you observe in people, nature and things around you that once you say it, others might agree with? Write statements like these:

> You can tell by the raised voices of people talking on their cell phones while they wait in line for movies or to make bank deposits that they are never really happy shooting the breeze.

> You can tell by the way students stare past their professors in front of them how little the world has changed.

> You can tell by the oversized plump plastic orange carts at wholesale shopping clubs how eager everyone is to display their sense of economy and their yuppie good taste all in the same trip.

Following Carlson's clever language tricks, you have probably made some hefty sparks fly. In journal speak, that's a full repayment against the debt of the blank page!

Lisa Shea's journaling example

"They're pretty, but you couldn't cook with them," Carlson writes about his thickening for the brew. You may be entertained by the sparks and pleased you got them down, exercising your writing muscle, but you may also feel you need to spend some time with the journal—filling the fireplace full of logs and kindling, the barbecue with charcoal and lighter fluid to do some cooking. Novelist Lisa Shea has found a way to do this by writing meditations on words.

In a journal entry dated March 4, 1995, Shea demonstrates some real home cooking by writing a meditation on the plant name "lovage," a meditation that serves up a whole meal on how it feels losing her marriage:

March 4, 1995

When I came across the word lovage in the newspaper this morning, in an article on English herbs, I thought of two other words—love and age—and right away I knew I wanted to write about these words, to put down something of their meaning, to see what I have learned from them, taken together and apart, in the eight months since my marriage ended.

I want to know where I am with love, and with age, and what is the proper fit of my heart, and how I will go on out of that need, out of all the knowing that I do not yet know.

Love first. Because it is harder, more ineffable, bigger, dumber, more wondrous, harder, truer, falser, faster, slower, not at all, harder, softer, softer, softer; it is unreliable, less and more, and never enough and baroque and italianate and South Brooklyn and Northampton and Washington and all in the mind and in the heart and especially in the groin.

Love is barbarous and cruel, chivalrous, utterly civilized, capable of killing you and you it. Love is backward, forward and I don't have to tell you it is upside-down. It is sincere, a sham, shamanistic, solipsistic, scruffulous and smart, stupid and shocking and still-born and somnolent and sublime.

Love is a lie. It is pure truth. It is a sickness, and in perfect health, till death do us part, partake, take apart. It is a small green park, a moat, a chimney, a purple rock. Love lies there, seducing you with its gorgeous hair and eyes, its muscled back.

Age. The thing we wear, our first skin, and into it and out of it we shrink and expand, elongate and contract, shrivel and stretch. Age carries us on its back, as we carry our children, and they us. It is newborn and unborn and reborn. It is the color of nails and eyelids and teeth, of the planet Saturn, of anything homemade, of wariness and pleasure and beat-up hope.

Age bears down as it flies up, coming round like sniper's fire and feathers, like olives and old underwear, touching our ear lobes, our ready loins. Age takes us and gives us back, always different, always the same. We can't walk away from it or toward it but only with it, as it stays and stays, making us real, forcing us with its brilliant, bullying, buffoonish ways to be who we are, and only that, thank God and Goddammit.

So there are love and age, and how they separate and combine, mysterious herbs in a strange garden, the worlds of these words dehiscent as I read in the paper of lovage and borage and fire and frost, as the days accumulate away from an ending that was large and long, full of love's terrible labor, the gorgeous, grotesque garden of our making and unmaking.

Shea writes that she continued to keep a journal with some lapses since she was in the eighth grade, keeping "a record of . . . preadolescent pains and fixations and especially, of increasingly sexual and subversive thoughts."

She says:

My journal writing has served primarily as a repository of secrets and experiences, a place where observations and opinions, feelings and facts intersect and entwine. I have used the journal to record daydreams and nightmares, wishes, fantasies, cruelties and conundrums, to relax and to scrutinize. It is where I tell the truth and the place where I fashion lies.

One of the many uses of the journal has been as a companion, a silent listener, an "other" to whom I can reveal myself without constraint. As a child, growing up Catholic, I went every week to confession. I think the habit of journal writing is, for me, connected to this early ritual act.

The entry March 4, 1995, is a meditation on love and age in the wake of my marriage having ended eight months earlier. The journal allows me to bring ideas that are buried to the surface and address them in a formal, expressive way. It is a quarry for everything else I write—fiction, nonfiction and poetry—and it is a shelter from those other works, no less from the world.

Keeping a journal is a form of mental and emotional exercise. It helps keep the mind limber and the soul supple, the better to get at the root of your own curiosities and obsessions as a writer.

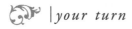 *your turn*

Here are some exercises to ensure you can mine that quarry, build that shelter, exercise the mind and the emotions, and do the cooking that writing requires.

1. Write down the names of plants you know, trees,

flowers, vegetables and shrubs. Cotoneaster, buddleia, potentilla and cornflowers come to me. Choose one from your
list—potentilla would be mine today—and begin writing
freely about what comes to your mind when you say the
name of this plant. Keep writing without stopping for ten
to twenty minutes. Remember that Shea starts many paragraphs by repeating "love" or "age." She introduces other
strong-sounding words to make her points in lists.

Taking off from her example, I might start a freewrite
like this:

> Potentilla, the name of a plant in my garden, the
> sound of potent and flotilla. I say the name of the
> plant in my garden and I seem to sail away somewhere
> with strength and virility. My days and my friends,
> my writing and my thoughts are good medicine. I
> think of the yellow flowers on the branches beside my
> front stairs, little stepping stones to my inner
> thoughts, vaccinations against forgetting the strength
> that has me celebrating each new day, each. . . .

2. "Age takes us and gives us back, always different, always the same . . . forcing us with its brilliant, bullying,
buffoonish ways to be who we are." Writers let words roll
off their tongues as a way of going on and getting deeper
and deeper into their thoughts, as a way of throwing a rope
down into the abyss and rappelling down. Try your hand
at this strategy by taking a word you are obsessed with, a
word you use often or a word that amuses you. Let words

flow because they sound right with the word you have chosen, and you will create just the rope you need to get to where you are going:

> Pimple. Pimples posit our walk through poisons each day, pockets full of how we go on, sometimes soft pillows for the tears that slide down our skin's canyons and slopes, and sometimes pebbles brought by a seagull a long way from beaches, dropped where they are stuck and out of place. Pimples pester, fester and saunter instead of healing. Pimples remember their places. Pimples erupt and reabsorb, pimples flower out of their own beds, and they remind us we can never be old enough not to get them, never be pure enough not to need their ways of cleansing.

Go back and see if you have said anything that interests you. Take off from whatever interests you in a ten- to twenty-minute freewrite. In mine, I would continue on about the cleansing. In what ways am I wrong to think I won't be sinful or incorrect anymore? That is the question I think I have written to in fooling around with the word "pimple." Now I can dive right in writing what comes to mind quickly:

> I am fifty-two and still I sometimes, not meaning to, overlook another's point of view, don't see it clearly because their words are different than words I'd use to say what they are saying. Their thinking is so

straight, I fly over it with my own circuitous thoughts. What is to be done to heal these ways? Bad days, how can I take the circle out of my thinking and hear the arrow of another point of view?

Be playful and don't worry about where you are going. Using the sounds of words you'll find out where that is. The writing is smarter than we are, my many teachers used to say. Trust that.

3. "Love is a lie. It is pure truth." Take an intangible: hate, joy, sorrow, imagination, frustration, beauty, success and failure, to name a few. Make two simple opposing statements using the word you choose. "Success is sweet. It is as bitter as unripe apples." Now give your word an ability to perceive like Shea does when she says love seduces. Personify your word further as Shea does when she says love has gorgeous hair and eyes and a muscled back. In my example, I might say, "Success lies in wait like my cat watching my toes wiggle under the covers. Its eyes remain unblinking; only its whiskers twitch. I know it will puncture my skin with its sharpened nails."

Now freewrite for ten to twenty minutes telling a little story or anecdote about a time you dealt with the notion you are writing about. I might write about the time I helped seventh-grade students perform the play *Our Town*, and despite the community's support and the students' joy and pride in their production, I was cast out of the fold by the other teachers in the school. They did not like an untenured teacher energizing things to a level higher than the one they were comfortable with.

Denise Levertov's journaling example

Sometimes, we don't want to write a long meditation, but we want to muse a little about our doings and readings. The late poet Denise Levertov was a master at using her journal to accomplish this as well as fill up her shopping bag:

> *9 December, 1994*
> *Rereading* Emma *with such delight. It seems perhaps the very best of Jane Austen, even better than* Pride and Prejudice. *'Mr. Knightly seemed to be trying not to smile; and succeeded without difficulty, upon Mrs. Elton beginning to talk to him.' In Volume III chapter iii she writes, 'Could a linguist, a grammarian, even a mathematician, have seen what she did . . . without feeling (etc.)? How much more must an imaginist, like herself, be on fire with speculation and foresight!—' What a wonderful term,* imaginist!

> *10 December, 1994*
> *. . . Richard Jones' good reading, during which he said he'd come to see that Rilke's 'You must change your life' was not about a once-and-for-all, romantic change but about the need for daily renewal and rebirth. Also he said, 'Poetry is my teacher,'—referring to the way that, once begun, a poem evolves its own story.*

27 December, 1994
San Diego
Savoldo's Temptation of St. Antony—*an unexpectedly Boschesque interpretation [for its period]. The 'temptations' in such pictures are not 'alluring' but rather are such symbols of disorder that I think the temptation is not so much a seduction as the magnetic abyss of a loss of faith in the prevalence of God's order, of justice and mercy—a loss of hope in Truth and Beauty. So it is very relevant to the contemporary—the terror that the horrors of the world are in the end what will prevail, 'more real' than anything else. The 'after the Holocaust, poetry is impossible' syndrome. St. Anthony resists, not without evident effort—asserting the reality of the ordered world seen at the left of the picture.*

Granacci's Stilllife *(some time before 1681) with its symbolism—the lizard and cricket at the bottom, the raffia unwinding on the Chianti bottle, the scale of dull to bright in color of butterflies' wings, the triumphant uprising of the red carnations, the last butterflies red and gold . . .*

A small 'non-Italian' yet wonderfully still and brooding Corot in which the architectural element grounds the silvery romance.

Reading Voyage Round My Room *in new New Directions edition (refound my French one just before I received it, after years!) The French Sterne. Also* Raj, *Gita Mehta. And rereading Okamura's* Awakening to Prayer.

27 March, 1995
Things I left out of Tesserae *(maybe to do some other time?):*

Bishop Breziando and the monkey muffs. Robert De Niro in the playground. Governor Rockefeller on 34th Street. Langston Hughes at Muriel's. Sonny Rollins at SVA. Haile Selassie at St. George's. 'The Venetian'—and the old man recounting 'Mireille'. . . Arrival at Brunnenberg in that 3-wheeler. Normal McLaren on the beach (Puerto V., or Barra, or Puerto Rico?). Daddy and 'Sixteen Pounds.' Etc! Oh, Paris: the old Russian anarchist with the goats, the non-excursion to Versailles, the Céline-style job, the day with the Spanish anarchists . . .

(Early 1980s)

NYC cop explaining to BBC interviewer: 'Any overt action on the part of this feller and I'm gonna shoot him.' Sports headline in English newspaper: 'An academic exercise fluently accomplished by Middlesex.' A nice comment on U.S. and British language use.

(Around 1958)

Held a black broad-bellied lizard in my hand. It eats flowers (likes dandelions). Have to support tail while holding. Janet may bring a blue-tongued skink home with her soon—it eats meatballs. Also a potto!

The new paint—how it made other things look shabby, but made beautiful objects more themselves.

October 9

The shadows of the lamp in evening sunlight.
The colors of the Indian corn.

Dedication of new PS41. Why do tears always spring to my eyes when I see kids perform their rehearsed bits at some such function? The photo of the N. African workman learning to read—same thing.

The pathos of anyone actually applying themselves to something for which they're liable to be crudely ridiculed while practising. Sense of human courage.

October 16
To the Frick Collection with Mitch. The sharp blue sky and clouds in the El Greco Expulsion from the temple—something of hope . . . The almost tender smile of Christ as he confidently advances. Rembrandt's face, its wisdom, its almost-about-to-smile look alongside its severe, judging, well-knowing look. The life coming from it, the awareness.

To walk the road in the Theodore Rousseau painting!

January 1959
Wallace Fowlie on Claudel: 'The universe as a text, to be deciphered.'

1959
Dream: the cowardly Seneschal, the Knight and his lady—they were arranging for a feast and the Seneschal was comically eager to so arrange that he had a place of safety and a possible way of escape if there was any trouble. The Knight or Lord and the Lady knew him of yore and exchanged mocking glances over his head. She wore a fur-trimmed robe, 14th century style. The wall—the great fireplace—the great door at the far end.

A strong sense that this was not a personal dream but a frag-
ment of the actual past suspended in time, into which I entered
briefly. The 'handles,' so to speak, by which I got in, were the
face of the blacksmith in The 7th Seal, *which resembled the*
Seneschal's, and the title of the Fernandel film we didn't see,
Seneschal the Magnificent. *And of course Sir Kay the Sene-*
schal, who was a coward. Nevertheless, I have the sense that I
was eavesdropping on the psychic image of an actual 14th
century moment.

May 5th
Brancusi, quoted in article in 'Arts': 'An artist generally has
the attitude that he must stop everything and get to work, that
work itself is something special, sacred, apart from life. On the
contrary, a man should work as he breathes, as he sweeps the
floor, easily and naturally, without thinking too much about
it.' (i.e., without thinking about the fact that he's doing it.)
'In fact, I can think of no better way of getting to work than
drifting into it after sweeping the floor and cleaning up. An
artist should always do his own chores.' Also: 'One's salvation
is decided within oneself. Those who allow themselves to be
drawn into competition are thereby allowing a degeneration of
their vital forces.'

May 29
The cat's broad neck and small head.

Ms. Levertov didn't recall keeping a journal until sometime in her late twenties; she wrote, ". . . but in my teens

I did fill a couple of large hardcover legal ledgers with copied-out excerpts from what I was reading, particularly poems." She wrote about her specific kind of journal keeping:

At certain periods later on I kept quite voluminous journals, particularly at a time when, under Jungian influence, I was meticulous about recalling and writing down my dreams. Even so, there would be large gaps. And at a certain point I began to feel I was living in order to dream and record my dreams, so I gave up even intermittent regularity and wrote in my journal only when I felt a particular urge to do so. Sometimes, however, I again felt a need for more regular journal keeping over a period of months. Often, when I'm traveling, my journal or notebook fills up almost exclusively with notes on paintings I've seen, since I visit art museums whenever I can, wherever I go; such notations help me revisualize what I've seen.

When I was doing the Ignatian Spiritual Exercises, I kept a separate daily notebook in that connection, while at the same time maintaining irregularly an ordinary journal. But ordinarily, notes on spiritual matters go into the same book as notes on things seen (in nature or art), quotes from current reading, dreams and often, the first drafts of poems. Unless specially memorable or important to me, any notations of public or private social events, movies or plays, or musical recitals (unless I have something very particular to say about them) and so forth don't usually go into a journal but may get a comment in my engagement book, like "Wonderful!" or "Very good evening." But I do list what I'm currently reading. . . .

. . . A writer's notebook is a way of keeping in touch with your inner life in the midst of the rush of daily preoccupations. . . . If a word haunts you, "out of nowhere," or a whole phrase, write it down. Ideas, likewise. . . . The value of the notebook is in the way writing such things down deepens our experience of them in that act itself—enriches our inner life, puts us in more intimate touch with ourselves.

᪪ |*your turn*

Ms. Levertov fed her mind and her spirit by reading, attending lectures and author events, and going to museums. To keep in touch with your inner life, emulate Ms. Levertov by doing these four exercises inspired from her musings and record keeping:

1. As Levertov reports doing in her December 9 entry, begin rereading a book you have already read. Make a statement about what you think of it so far this time around. Quote a small portion of the book that engages you, maddens you or otherwise supports your statement. Now take a term from that portion of the book and apply it to the writer and her writing. You will surprise yourself with your enthusiasm for your point of view!

2. Go to a lecture by an expert or a reading by an author. These are open to the public at universities, colleges and bookstores, among other venues. You can also find experts participating in online chats. After you attend, write in your journal at some length about the event, remembering to quote several things the expert or author said that hooked you, made you think or raised a lot of questions. Write about how you think this information will influence you in the coming days.

3. Go to a museum. Stand before an exhibit or a painting or an artifact. Describe what you see and what you make of the philosophy of the artist or exhibit creator. Do you agree or disagree? Write about that. You can also imagine yourself agreeing and then disagreeing. Next, write about both points of view. Finally, write a paragraph about what you are reading currently. Add the music you are interested in and what movies and plays you have recently seen. Think about any connections between the museum exhibit, your thoughts and the impact of the readings, music, movies and plays.

4. Find some words that inspire you. You might come across them in reading, in broadcast media or in hearing others say them in conversation. Write the words down. Tell who said them or where you found the words you quoted. Then, write for a short while about what you think of the quote and how its meaning might operate in your life and the lives of people you know.

As an example I began:

> Ms. Levertov's short entry, "the cat's broad neck and small head," makes me think about support and intelligence, the continuity between them. It makes me think how comical it is that a human's head sits on a narrow pedestal while the cat's head has a lot of muscular support. I . . .

May your journal entries be the substantial muscles that support your interesting, very alert thoughts!

passions for projects and processes

M any writers enjoy making journal entries about their progress with projects or pieces of writing. You might want to consider making regular entries using your work, hobbies, projects or missions as subject material. If you are coaching soccer, leading a Cub Scout or Brownie troop, planning a wedding or setting a goal to be accepted to graduate school, you have something to write about. If you raise orchids, breed cats, restore houses or classic cars, or quilt, you have things to say about how these things are done and how you know you have done them correctly. If you are a team leader at work or trying to convince your boss of something, you have plans, insights and mistakes to write about. When you write about processes that you have a passion for, you will find that your entries contain an array of terms and images, lists, instructions, names of materials and goals. These specifics feed your writer's brain, and you may start to see how what you are engaged in doing contains metaphors for how you or others live. The following three authors all use journal entries to keep track of the activities they love.

Maxine Kumin's journaling example

The poet Maxine Kumin has kept a journal intermittently over twenty or thirty years. In her entries, she observes seasonal changes on her farm, and she writes about horses, since she owns and raises them. She says her journal entries are "grist for the mill in one way or another." She has written that in reading, she's always been drawn to journals and letters:

. . . they feed the voyeur in me as I suspect they do in so many other writers. I am most keenly interested in women's journals and letters—Plath, Sexton, Louise Bogan, Woolf, of course. But also John Cheever's, James Agee's and so on.

Keeping a journal is a highly individual and eclectic occupation. . . . It's a good habit to get into, like five-finger exercises at the piano.

In the following sample entry, Ms. Kumin writes about a guided tour she took of a thoroughbred breeding farm:

May, 1993
Pobiz is wondrous strange. On a free Sunday morning during an arduous gig in central Texas, Chester Critchfield, a retired biologist who bounces along jauntily on the balls of his

sneakered feet, conveys me on a guided tour of the native flora and fauna. An enthusiast who would rather spend an hour watching a flower open than chase a golf ball across the ubiquitous greens, Chester is vividly at one with his environment. Behind his house where the land drops down to the creek he has excavated a sizable pond, lined it with limestone bricks and stocked it with Japanese carp exotically striped and stippled orange, black and white. Several ugly catfish patrol the bottom and a healthy school of tilapia rise to snap at the pellets he broadcasts over the surface. Tilapia, he informs me, are the biblical fish of the Sea of Galilee. He thinks they and the carp would do well in my sheep-pasture fire pond, a saucer some fifty feet in diameter, possibly eight feet deep at the center.

As we cross the adjoining meadow I see my first loggerhead shrike under Chester's tutelage: it's a savage little bird of prey that impales its quivering catch on thorns then retrieves and devours them at leisure. I had always expected a shrike to be bigger than a bluejay, at least. It makes up in ferocity for what it lacks in stature.

We drive out to a huge Thoroughbred breeding farm where Chester has made arrangements for a guided tour. Ken Quirk, the resident vet, is one of the most gracious hosts I've come across in these often sterile and forbidding establishments. We arrive at an easy rapport in spite of the hard night he's been through—a leased mare bred last summer and then sent home to her owner who failed to have her ultrasounded early in the pregnancy was returned to them a few weeks ago for supervised foaling. Last night she delivered full-term twins, in itself a rarity, as the mare's uterus seldom provides an eleven-month-

long hospitable environment for twins. The filly is near death, sedated with Valium to control her seizures. She is a "wobbler" or "dummy foal," a condition caused by inflammation of brain tissue. They are trying to reduce the swelling with DMSO infusions, but it doesn't look good. The colt has a better chance. He's been up, with assistance. He has a sucking reflex but is not yet able to swallow. Both are being fed four ounces of colostrum from the mother, milked out and delivered via stomach tube every two hours. The vet's heroic measures put our own dozen travails with dams and foals into perspective. Of course I am fascinated.

143 bred mares here, the newest still in open pens under a high roof, which provides good ventilation. But with so many so close, there's a higher incidence of infection than, say, on the family farm. With us, pre-delivery precautions consist of taking out the old bedding down to sand and gravel, liming the area, and then rebedding. When the mare actually gives birth—or shortly before she does so, if we're alert to it—we switch from sawdust to straw, to reduce the possibility of a newborn inhaling dust particles and/ or ammonia fumes from the urine. One of our mares, a greedy old lady, eats straw, which complicates things a bit. We've sat out a few tough nights with mares whose distended udders made them reluctant to give suck but we've never—so far—had a bacterial or any other postnatal infection.

It's still showery and cool here although spring is well advanced. The redbuds are finished flowering and are putting out new leaves. Older colts and their mothers are turned out on pasture in groups of six or eight. These oldtime broodmares coexist comfortably. 15 stallions cover this herd; retired stakes winners, sons and latter-day descendants of Seattle Slew and Native Dancer. The stallions' life is far from enviable, however. All of them are confined to box stalls as we tour, though Dr. Quirk says they are usually turned out. It's Sunday and Sunday is a down-day at this farm. One stalwart morose stud is wearing a muzzle. We can see where he tears himself up biting in frustration. He covered 80 mares last year, which seems an extraordinary figure. It would be a kindness to castrate him and let him have an outdoor life free of his gonads, but he's a money-maker.

They raise ostriches here too, but the birds are setting now and can't be viewed. A fertile egg is worth as much as $1500— so much for any fantasies of breeding ostriches! Tilapia sound more reasonable.

Two days later I am driven in a stretch limousine, complete with liquor bar and tv, back to the airport for a predawn departure. A first for me, the limo, but I chafe, thinking how wasteful and ostentatious it is.

I loved the carp. They live, Chester told me, as much as 90 years. You too. Chester. Be well.

your turn

Using Ms. Kumin's example, create field trips for yourself every once in a while to foster one or more of your interests, then write about these trips in your journal. Ms. Kumin includes lots of details and technical information learned on her guided tour. She knows the names and characteristics of birds and fish new to her. She has learned about the life of a stallion, the problems of a birthing mare and what is being done for the mare. Her journal entry records the event of visiting the farm with Chester Critchfield. It is evidence of this poet's observant being and her love of detail about animals, livestock and those who care for them.

Instead of giving you three different prompts inspired by Ms. Kumin's journal entry, I urge you to do this sort of journal entry over and over as you wish, since each time you make a "field trip" you will have a new adventure to write about. Use the ideas I share below. Feel free, of course, to customize them to fit your needs or make up ideas for yourself that serve your needs better. The important thing is that the place you visit feeds your interest in a particular area and provides you with some kind of "guide" who will teach you new information that you can then write about in a journal entry:

- If you love to cook, visit markets filled with exotic food. Talk to vendors about a specific food-related topic.
- If you are a baker, go to bakeries and bakery supply stores and do the same.
- If you love sports, go to a store that sells the equipment needed, and talk at length with a clerk or a customer who seems to know a lot.
- If electronics is a current passion, do this exercise at a store that sells electronics equipment.
- If your passion is cars, there are lots of showrooms and mechanics shops that you can visit to do this exercise.
- If you love to read, go to a well-stocked bookstore and visit each aisle carefully.

- If you bike, go on a ride you haven't done led by someone knowledgeable about the area, or stop and talk to someone who lives or works there.
- If you garden, visit botanical gardens, working farms or nurseries to complete this exercise.

Once you have decided on your trip, *visit, learn and reflect* as Ms. Kumin does. Write a journal entry that tells how you got there, who led you around or offered information, what was going on, what you observed, what you learned, what you overheard, how you got home and what you hope for the people you met. In the middle of the entry, center on something technical you learned or reviewed, and write about it in detail. How will this knowledge affect you? Write about that.

David Mas Masumoto's journaling example

Sometimes journal keepers devote entries over a span of time to one process they are engaged in. The nonfiction writer David Mas Masumoto once kept a journal about journal keeping. He wrote seven entries over three months, answering questions about what makes a journal important, what he puts into his journal, how it functions for him and how the journal comes to an end sometimes:

March 8
A journal about keeping a journal. This could be dangerous,

venturing into the private world of a writer and exposing a vein. But isn't that what journals are all about? Another danger lies in analyzing journal writing—the writer becomes too self-conscious, overly critical and the words loose their freedom. For me, that's what keeping a journal is about: thinking freely.

I've read many types of journals. I've tried lots of ways to keep a journal. I don't have a favorite journal writer and some of the best material I've read is about keeping a journal—or as in Joan Didion's case, "On Keeping a Notebook" (from Slouching Towards Bethlehem).

Because I farm, my field work is often woven into my journals. But do records on when the peaches first bloom or the grape shoots peak out at the spring sun or the early signs of worms in my peaches—do they belong in my journal?

Yes and no. They are part of what makes a journal important—a documentation of where you were and what you felt at a specific time and place. But do worms and metaphors belong on the same page? I've written some of my best stories about worms—but I keep a different type of farm journal in addition to my writing journal. No one said I couldn't have more than one.

March 17

Journals capture my ideas, my emotions, the smell of the mowed grasses, the taste of a wildflower lemon stalk, the images from the farmhouse porch on a cool spring morning. My farm journals do the same; they record my feelings about a spring storm on peach blossoms or the fear of invisible diseases growing on my grapes.

Writing and farming share a common tie—neither is done well by using formulas. Good stories are not based on recipes, a juicy peach cannot be grown by following "how to" books. Nor does technology automatically improve my work. Riveting characters and moving themes are not created by word processors and new software; bigger machines and new chemicals do not equate to better produce.

So I write and farm drawing from experiential knowledge. I need to dirty my hands to write about farm work. I need to feel the tightening of stomach muscles when a dark storm approaches in order to understand a sense of helplessness as I bow before nature.

My journals take many forms. Some are scribbled notes I write while on a tractor and then jam into a file folder. Later I'll pull out the pieces of paper like leaves in a family album, each tells a story of a moment in time and the emotions captured in the words and shaky handwriting. I keep another journal of one-page entries with headings that sound like short story titles. Some will grow into manuscripts such as a journal entry entitled "Five Worms" that later became a story about the meaning of finding worms in your peaches and my learning to live with nature.

My journals allow me to integrate my ideas with who I am. My words are not removed from the real and everyday. And that is precisely what I strive for in my stories.

April 8

I do not write in my journal every day, though I am disciplined enough to write daily. On days where the words cease to flow or my thoughts are jumbled, I can return to my journals.

*They help soothe and calm and provide a forum to "think out"
ideas and issues.*

*My journals often do not make sense. I have a rule: there
can be no wrongs in my journals. I misspell words frequently,
use wrong verb tenses, create sentence fragments. I can check
the facts later, I can verify quotes some other time. Some
thoughts ramble, others remain disconnected and out of place,
I enjoy nonlinear thinking, jumping from idea to idea without
worrying about how they may be connected and coherent.*

*What's important is to get it out on paper, to commit feelings
to words, to write and capture the creative spirit. I seek a
freedom of expression, for no one will read these journals verba-
tim, my words are not intended for writing teachers or editors.
No one will ever write in red ink "Who cares?" over my words.
I care and that's all that matters.*

*Journals provide me with the raw materials to work with.
I'll write about the frustrations of farm life and the precarious
relationship when working with nature. I'll write about
screaming at dark thunderclouds as my delicate peaches hang
on my trees. Does it help to shout at a storm? Yes, because when
I write about it, I realize how silly I must have appeared
while doing a farmer's anti-rain dance. I'll explore the amazing
power of the human spirit to rationalize events. If there was
no downpour, I'll claim my pleas worked; if it hails, I'll assume
nature is merely teaching me a lesson about humility.*

*In my journals I explore everyday life. The entries allow me
access into my thoughts and emotions. I increase my odds at
successful writing by making myself available—my journals
provide me with opportunity.*

April 25
Poetry and prose.
Some of my journal entries are written in the form of single-line entries.

I like to think of these as poetic prose.
Like good poetry,
the single-line format invites reflection.

Here's how it works.
I begin with a single word or phrase.
Then I brainstorm and am soon bulging with thoughts,
I need to get them out before I lose one.
That's when the ease and simplicity of a journal shines.
My writing resembles a random list of ideas.
Some stand independent of each other,
some are clearly connected,
but they all reflect how I think at the moment,
complete with the excitement of creative energy.

Later I'll add more details
Some ideas blossom into longer stories.
Others need to be clarified,
I bundle the thoughts into a package
that I can ponder when I'm out in the fields.

A few remain loners,
I'll wrestle with them
and try to figure out why they were even mentioned.

I seek to establish a series of connections,
thoughts that relate to each other

and give life to one another.
I search for those meaningful connections.

April 30
I often reread my old farm journals, retracing my footsteps over familiar ground while renewing past friendships. The passing of time contributes to a refreshing perspective—I no longer have high ownership of my words and ideas.

Why was I so preoccupied about summer pruning of peaches in '92? Did it really make a difference when I found some worms in my peaches? "Where I was" helps orient me to "where I am now." Journals date me because my memory too easily lies.

Future stories often begin in the passages of my farm journals. An old neighbor drops by and shares his invention for drying grapes into raisins. My nine-year-old daughter drives the tractor by herself—my little girl is now big and strong enough to push down the clutch—a modern-day rite of passage for farm kids. We fertilize a young orchard as a family working together; we all have our jobs as we nourish life for the future. Raw ideas for good stories like an artist's sketches.

In my journals I show what once happened so I can later reread the passages and learn. The bad writing will reek terribly; I'll be amazed I even wrote such garbage. The good entries will ring with honesty and they will be fun to revisit.

May 4
Why do I keep a journal? Partially for instant gratification. I like seeing my thoughts put into words; I enjoy the sense of accomplishment when I complete a good writing session.

Occasionally the entry becomes an instant first draft for a manuscript.

Let me share two examples. First, my story, "Snapshot, 1944," began when I found an old photograph of my uncle's funeral during the relocation of Japanese Americans from their homes during World War II. The first line in my journal became the first line of the story, "I stare at the silent and still faces, expressions frozen in a snapshot." The story grew directly from my journal as I explored the meaning of this photograph, trying to make sense of a moment in history when my family, because they were Japanese Americans, were uprooted and imprisoned for four years behind barbed wire. The raw emotions of a journal entry provides the underpinning for a story that won a writing award, then appeared in my collection of short stories, Silent Strength, and will soon be republished in a "storytelling" anthology.

Second, because I write mostly nonfiction, many passages evolve into essays and may find their way into newspaper op-ed sections. I wrote one particular piece about a wonderful-tasting peach that lacks cosmetic "good looks" and becomes homeless in the marketplace. This was during the middle of a summer harvest; I had lost thousands of dollars and thousands of boxes of these peaches sat unsold in cold storage. My essay, published in the LA Times, was based on my journal entry: "The flesh of my peaches is so juicy that it oozes down your chin. The nectar explodes in your mouth. The fragrance enchants your nose, a natural perfume that could never be captured . . ."

This story then took on a life of it's own. From journal entry to the LA Times *to now, a book entitled* Epitaph for a Peach: Four Seasons on My Family Farm. *Good things can happen with our journals.*

May 21
Soon my journal writing will become lean. Farm work takes center stage, 80 acres of vines and trees demand my attention. I am torn by the dilemma, to stay inside and write or to go outside and prepare for the harvests. A writer must do both, no? But like farming, my journals will be here for the next season and if I'm fortunate, for the season after that too.
Postscript: Every family needs a writer, a family journal writer. Who else can document and save family histories? Who else can pass on the voices and characters for the next generation? Stories honor the legacy of a family for an audience of the living and those not yet born.

🐦 | *your turn*

The following journal-keeping ideas are inspired by the way Masumoto journals about his journaling process, the way he puts down ideas about mastery and the way he reports experimenting with different approaches to journal keeping.

1. Commit to keeping at least six journal entries over a period of time about a process you are engaged in—grieving; making new friends after a move or a job change; buying, remodeling or painting a house; planting a garden; raising children; planning a wedding, holiday party or event; learning to scuba dive, play the piano, play tennis or dance.

Each time you sit down to write an entry begin with one of these questions:

- Why am I doing this activity?
- What am I learning from the process?
- What do I hope will happen because I am doing this?
- What is hard about it?
- What surprises am I encountering along the way?
- What would I want to tell someone else about this process?

Write in detail, as Masumoto does, including memories and anecdotes.

2. Here is a journal entry Masumoto wrote when he wasn't journaling about journaling, but about tending his fruit trees. Notice his attention to detail and process:

The Shape of Trees   July 1994

I need help in shaping young trees.
Their young shape stays with you for years.
Mistakes are not corrected,
they plague me like a wound.

Not a scar but a living wound.

That's not quite true.
If they are a wound,
I would cut out the tree and start over.

They plague me with their history.
In their shape I see the past
and the effect on the present
as well as the future.

Young trees need to be trained with tight centers.

Their vase shape needs to be rigid and
much more upright than you'd expect.

The reason why is because over the years, possibly decades,
the weight of the fruit will gradually pull the branches
downwards,
stretching the limbs downwards
and opening up the vase.

The tree maintains an upright structure,
not sagging limbs heavy with harvest.

That image is great for poetry and painting
but bad for farming.

Like stretch marks,
sagging limbs do not return to their previous position
after bearing a heavy crop.
They will sag and continue to sag the rest of their life.

I can rope them to tighten the vase
but the wood will never be as strong and sound.

I need to think: structurally sound.

Think of something you have to master or have mastered. Write about it as if you were writing a poem by creating stanzas with varying line lengths and numbers of lines per stanza. Once you have accomplished this, you may find as Masumoto did, that you can come to an ending that is indeed poetic—some wisdom earned from the images and details you included in your stanzas.

3. "My journals take many forms," Masumoto writes. "Some are scribbled notes I write while on a tractor and then jam into a file folder. Later I'll pull out the pieces of paper like leaves in a family album." And he tells us, "I keep another journal of one-page entries with headings that sound like short story titles." Try your hand at both these kinds of journals.

Over a period of time, in addition to the journaling you are doing regularly in your journal, commit to writing brief thoughts, feelings and observations on scraps of paper— napkins, bank deposit slips and "while you were out" message pad paper, for example. Store these scraps in a drawer, file folder, box or envelope. One day, after your storage place has many scraps in it, take them out and read them. Write a journal entry about what you think as you read what you had jotted down over days and weeks.

Next, take some journal-writing days to keep the one-page entries Masumoto is talking about. Fill a page but no more and then read over what you have written. Give your entry a title from an image or an action you have included in the entry. After you have done this many times, reread your entries and titles, and see if you want to write longer on any particular one. The title may help you feel as if you have more to say.

William Matthews's journaling example

The late poet William Matthews wrote that a journal "encourages scrappiness. Things needn't be finished, just stored, the way one might 'store' a five-dollar bill in a trouser pocket in the closet for two weeks only to discover it smugly the next time the trousers get worn." In the following entry, you'll get to follow his mind as he thinks about the process of writing a poem for his son's wedding and as he collects some scraps that will help him generate a poem rather than lead to an idea:

A morally sentimental 1968 rhyme: Nazi/ROTC.

Is it more interesting to distinguish between different levels of evil than between different levels of good, or just easier?
As a boy, I thought "good" was monolithic, and so I remember vividly the first time I heard the phrase "too kind." Who spoke of whom? Where? When? I don't remember. But the monolith began to crumble. Some loose pebbles, some rocks, next boulders, and then an avalanche.

White southern women: "She's too kind."
Urban black boys: "He's bad."

Irony is not a defense against emotion. It's an emotion about the relationship between words and emotion.

But then, emotion is a poor defense against irony. "Only a man with a heart of stone could read the death of Little Nell without laughing." (Oscar Wilde)

German food critic: "The wurst is full of passionate intensity."

Of course it's a dumb joke. Are jokes about being smart? Are smart jokes about being dumb?

Sebastian has asked me to give—to reinvent—one of the traditional blessings for his wedding to Ali.

I've who've blessed my marriages with divorce
as a man shoots a broken-legged horse.

An uncouplet.

I get #7, which lists the ten shades of joy. A thrilling phrase, "ten shades of joy," but how dull they turn out to be, striding up the ramp in pairs not to the Ark but to the Love Boat:

bridegroom and bride
mirth and exultation
pleasure and delight
love and fellowship
peace and friendship.

The problem of course may lie somewhat in the translation. They make redundant couples, like legal phrases:

intents and purposes
will and testament.

Of course marriage and contract law are themselves a couple.

But where's the breathlessness, the giddiness, the risk, the thrill and terror of vow-making? Eclipsed by all those abstract nouns.

Re-invent traditional ceremonies and Who may wind up absent? The deity formerly known as Yahweh.

But here's the recurring problem poets face. The forms bristle with rust. Throw them wholly out and you've asked yourself to start from prose and make a poem. But if you're not suspicious of them and intelligently combative, they'll write your poem not for you, but instead of you.

The purpose of the forms is to raise talk above babble, and the purpose of "talk" is to tether the severities of the forms to the mess of emotional life. It's a two party system, and each party needs a loyal opposition.

Wouldn't it be easy to scrawl a journal entry in which I describe the relationship between "the forms" and "talk" as a mixed marriage, which would suggest why I, a deracinated WASP, will give the seventh blessing at a Jewish wedding?

Yes, as Nixon said, but it would be wrong.

Only a very great writer, Nabokov said in a related context, could resist such a temptation.

Well then, I won't do it.

The forms represent their own history and the "talk" represents this singular instance in the history.

William Matthews also wrote that:

. . . a reason to keep a journal is to stumble upon scraps long after one first meets them in their own contexts. It's easier to wonder "Now, what could I make from that?" if one can no longer remember very precisely what someone else had made from it. . . .

And Matthews pointed out that:

. . . Roethke's notebooks, in David Wagoner's beautifully edited version of them, *Straw for the Fire,* were used that way. Apparently he'd weed them each year, throwing out what no longer sparked. A few entries survived a dozen or more such cullings before Roethke put them to some use we can identify from his poems . . .

Roethke's was not a "scrapbook," with its hope to preserve something of the past, but a collection of scraps that yearn to be changed from their illusory current form into something else, something future. . . .

Illustrating what he means about using the journal to store bits and pieces, Matthews wrote:

I thought: "Ten Shades of Joy" will be ten stanzas, of course, of ten lines each. Pentameter, natch. Perhaps each stanza might conclude with a couplet as an instance of knot-tying. "Ten Shades of Joy."

The two lines I thought might become ⅓₀ of "Ten Shades
of Joy" became part of an altogether differently scaled poem
than the one I proposed to myself then:

The Bar at The Andover Inn   May 28, 1995

The bride, groom (my son), and their friends gathered
somewhere else to siphon the wedding's last
drops from their tired elders. Over a glass
of Chardonnay I ignored my tattered,
companionable glooms (This took some will:
I've ended three marriages by divorce
as a man shoots his broken-legged horse),
and wished my two sons and their families
something I couldn't have, or keep, myself.
The rueful pluck we take with us to bars
or church, the morbid fellowship of woe—
I'd had my fill of it. I wouldn't mope
through my son's happiness or further fear my own.
Well, what instead? Well, something else.

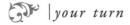 *|your turn*

William Matthews once compared the way he kept a journal to the "way a cook might tend a good strain of yeast or mother-of-vinegar." I think that means to treasure and store the living organism and to introduce it into recipes and baked goods. Here are three exercises you can use to try your hand at doing this:

1. Go back into journal entries you have already made. Pluck out five words or phrases (a group of words with no verb). Now imagine you are writing horoscopes for friends. Use one of the words or phrases in each horoscope.

2. Go back through your journal entries again. Pick out five sentences that appeal to you. Imagine you are writing affirmations for yourself inspired by the sentences. Add words or change the word order to make the affirmations meaningful.

3. Choose ten phrases from your journal. Write each on a scrap of paper, fold each scrap and drop it in a hat, jar, bowl or basket. Each day for five days, pick out one piece of paper. Do a ten- to twenty-minute freewrite beginning with the phrase you have chosen. Whenever you get stuck, write the phrase into your entry again and continue writing with whatever pops into your head after that. If you have to, keep writing the phrase over and over until you find something to say. Of course, something to say always arrives.

May writing in your journal about passions and hobbies and processes you are engaged in lead you to new understandings about the importance of what you are doing!

write letters to your loves

Many people feel they access and develop better ideas and thinking when they address their thoughts in letter form to someone else, whether or not they plan to send the letter. There is something about having certain audiences that helps writers feel more comfortable about where to start, what to include and how to shape experience. Thinking of certain people as an audience helps some writers write about particular topics that they might not address or explore otherwise. Novelist and nonfiction writer Anne Lamott has written that when she starts a novel, she begins by thinking of it as a gift to someone she knows would especially enjoy it.

Your journal keeping can be enhanced by entries in the form of letters. Following are journal entries and thoughts about them by three contemporary writers.

Pam Houston's journaling example

Pam Houston has written that she "never wrote more flu-idly, more excitedly, more directedly and more honestly" than in her love letters:

And since I seem to be always in love with somebody, since I am driven in my life and my work most strongly by desire, and since I can scarcely tell the difference between desire for the word and desire for the one, I began writing letters at the end of most days to some named beloved.

Sometimes I send the letter to the person whose name is on the top of it, and sometimes not. Sometimes the events I describe in the letter have actually happened, and sometimes not. The named recipient is most often real, though occasionally imaginary, and he is almost always male, because when one woman writes to another, she is able to leave so much out.

These letters contain most of the significant incidents, real and imagined, that make up the fabric of my life. . . .

The following three letters are from Houston's collection of love letters, each of them written roughly a year apart. This kind of letter writing serves as her journal:

Dear G—,

It is, in fact, called "breaking horses," and the reason it is called that is because the term was invented by a man. The man believed, wrongly, that he was capable of breaking the horse's spirit, of removing all that was wild from her, and he also believed, even more wrongly, that breaking her was the only way he could hold her, when of course, exactly the opposite was true. That man would be the first to tell you that the horse was only valuable to him when she was strong and free and responded to him out of respect and love and dedication. The minute he "broke" her, he would say (though he'd be wrong, she allowed herself to be broken . . . which is really like saying she broke herself) he lost interest in her and turned her into a dude horse that old ladies and kids could ride. But of course you know all this.

Let me tell you what happened today. C— was bent on going riding, and even though this is the city, it is also Texas, so we looked in the phone book and found a dude ranch and signed ourselves up for a three hour ride. C— rode a feisty little quarter horse called Charlotte, and I rode a big rangy thoroughbred/Tennessee Walker cross named Paul. Our wrangler's name was James and he was young and just about as Texan as you can get. And of course we signed papers and everything that said we wouldn't run the horses, but I know C— better than that, and we weren't twenty minutes into the ride when James made the mistake of going around a different side of a little stand of pines than we did and C— seized the moment he couldn't see us and belted her horse and we took off at a flat gallop across the top half of this four hundred and some acre cattle ranch.

A quarter horse is the best horse to have on a trail because she is strong and smart and basically willing to do what you ask her. What a thoroughbred is good at is putting his head down and running for the finish line, throwing care and caution and sense to the wind, setting his jaw and running, through or around or over whatever might get in his way. It's not his fault. We've bred him for it. And there is nothing I've ever done in my life that is as exhilarating, nothing that is so equally and completely frightening and magical than being on the back of a thoroughbred when he's in turbodrive. It's as smooth as a Cadillac convertible and much faster. It was the first recreational bargain I made with death, and one of the few I hope to keep making for as long as I live. But I've gotten off track here.

The day went a lot like that. Ten minutes of walk/trot pleasantness and then C— would bring Charlotte up to where I was and our horses would start bumping shoulders and I would turn and look at James and catch just the hint of a smile or a shake of his head and that was all we needed to be off again. Anyway, what I wanted to tell you about was the training, the lessons that took place between me and . . . Paul. The first time Paul took off on me, I was really scared. He took off like only a thoroughbred can, and I didn't know him, or the tack I was using, didn't know the terrain. I tried every trick I know to stop him (and I know them all). Constant pressure, intermittent pressure, I tried to turn him hard in a tight circle, tried shouting whoa whoa whoa at every possible voice level, tried even to kick him to attention (very poor horsemanship), and finally, after crossing three stream beds, clattering over two very nasty rock outcroppings, and shaving off about fifteen trees' branches with various parts of my body, I found a big canyon wall to run Paul into.

"Don't let that horse put his head down on ya," James said when he caught up to us that first time, "That horse puts his

head down, and you're just fucked." The second time we took off I played it a little different. I let him run as fast as he wanted until we got to a place that was steep and rocky. And then I hauled back on the reins one time, said Whoa once loud and sat back hard in the saddle. Paul stopped on a dime.

After that we came to a big open meadow. James said we couldn't go down there because it was the horses' winter pasture and they would get a little crazy in it, and I asked if I could go down for ten minutes by myself and work with Paul. I went down into the meadow and galloped him around in tight tight circles, but every time he'd stop fighting me, I'd drop the reins a little, and let him make the circle just a little more wide. I talked to him with my legs the whole time too asking for the gallop, and then asking for control (not my control, of course, but his, asking him to control his own gallop), showing him that asking for the speed and asking for control are not opposites, that they can be the same question asked with one movement of the leg, and you see that's why the legs are so important because in the same movement they ask for something from the horse, they also make a promise. They say you can trust me. They say I'm asking you to gallop with me, but I'm also telling you at every second that I'm right here with you to help you have the courage to gallop. The horse holds the rider up, it's true, but the rider holds the horse . . . in, or together. This is especially true when a horse and rider are out alone, because horses are herd animals and they need that constant contact of the leg then much more than most riders know.

Before too long we were galloping big circles around the whole meadow.

C— told me that the whole time we were down there James was saying "Any second now Paul's going to come flying over that hill dragging Theresa behind him." And I did let him out as we ran the last length of the field back to where C— and James were standing. But I wasn't hanging on for my life anymore. I was flying along right with him.

It was, from then on, one of the best rides ever on a horse I didn't know. And we did give James a really big tip.

And of course we are talking here about the ability of the trainer to teach, and the horse's ability to learn, as well as the trainer's ability to learn and the horse's ability to teach, and that is what makes horseback riding different from tennis or skiing, that there are two wills constantly engaged and those four learning situations are always and must be at every moment inextricable. And of course a horse tests his trainer, he tests her every minute, he reads her fears straight through her body like no human being ever could, he senses any momentary inattention and capitalizes on it. He sometimes pretends to be much less intelligent than he is, he walks into a hole or gets caught up in barbed wire, and I don't know why exactly. Maybe he likes watching her hands gently separate the barbs from his fetlocks . . . maybe he recognizes this as a tremendous act of love.

And of course they talk to one another, and most days they reach an understanding, and he becomes more human and she more equine, which doesn't take all that much becoming, because if she didn't have an equine spirit she wouldn't have become a horse trainer, and if he didn't have a human sensibility, he wouldn't be her chosen horse. And she does get tired, but not of him, or even of the training, but of falling down all the time in the same place. And though he's been tricked (not by her, but by something bigger, some universal law of order questionable but stronger than them) into believing that she's the one who's holding the lunge line, the simple laws of nature are that because of the different ways they are put together, one well enough placed kick can break her arm into nineteen pieces. And the one thing he really understands about her (and its both the reason he sometimes bucks her off, and the reason he'll walk through fire for her) is that what she wants most of all, what all the years of training have shown her, is the possibility of never again needing to use the whip.

Did I tell you that Jerry Jeff Walker signed my blonde leather coat? Did I tell you about Gruene, Texas and the oldest dance hall in the state? Did I tell you that in everything I see that moves . . . me . . . in the young girl at the grunge bar with magenta hair and ten nose rings, in the tall young blues singer in a band called Joe Teller who wailed into the microphone and wrapped his arms around it like an invisible woman and then walked off stage saying "I hate this fucking six string, I hate this fucking club, and I hate all you fucking people," in the third verse of Mr. Bojangles, in the deep set lines on Jerry Jeff's life-worn face, in the paler lines of clouds in the sky last night behind a lone Texas windmill, in the scrubby cedars and naked grey rocks of the canyons of the triple creek ranch, in the first surprise of speed in sixteen hands of horseflesh underneath me, in the slowing of that same horse, in the giving in. In all of these things and at every moment, I see my love for you.

P—

Ohhhhhh S—,

I am living today in some other reality. Some half lit space of fever and hallucination and flu. I'm unsure whether its day or night, in my head, you know, but all I need to do is look out the window and see that it's day. I read the script of the Good-bye Girl . . . and this I hesitate to admit even to you . . . cried continuously from about page 68 on. Nothing like snappy, overclever, utterly unbelievable dialogue to really open me up, heart and soul.

I pause here, unsure what to tell you next. Do I begin by describing the writing I've been doing, by telling you what pure unadulterated pleasure (and of course the necessarily accompanying pain) I have found these last weeks reimmersing myself in writing according to no one's agenda but my own, remembering that process from years ago where I sat down and just wrote the thing . . . the story or image or scene or thought that I had to write, and then just sat there to see what happened then, how the seeing what happened became what was thrilling. That's what all the nonfiction has taken away from me, the screenplay too . . . they have their own variety of seeing what happens, but it doesn't touch the freedom of this other project, that can go anywhere and do anything and be any length and shape itself into any form it likes; poem, letter, chapter, story. It asks so much more of me, demands it, and unlike the others, I have to enter it not knowing if I am up to the task, not knowing whether or not I will succeed, whether or not I will, God forbid, waste time.

Or should I begin by telling you I spent part of today with one of the most delightful human beings I've met in recent memory . . . he was articulate, gentlemanly, quite handsome, and four years old. Maybe, the most wonderful thing on earth is introducing a child to a horse for the very first time . . . and in this case it was doubly wonderful, because not only was Deseo Sam's first horse, but Sam was Deseo's first child. His mom, L—, is one of my students, and he and I hit it off instantly when he came racing into class one day, skidded to a stop in front of me, looked me up and down and said, "No way Mom, she's not a real teacher." To say Sam and Deseo delighted in each other would be a tragic understatement.

Deseo was soft and encouraging and precisely the right amount of playful . . . Sam was . . . well . . . soft and encouraging and precisely the right amount of playful. And the two moms, pride running off of us like water . . . we scarcely needed to be there at all.

Or should I begin instead with you and what's on my mind today concerning you, which is how very happy I am that you know me, as well as you seem to, that you know what my mind does with the things you say as well as I know exactly where Deseo's mind goes, not during, but in the few seconds after a mountain bike passes, and you know how to wrap your arms around that space, exactly how to rub its neck.

Or should I begin with my sighting of this bumper sticker near the Oakland Airport: Visualize Whirled Peas.

I think so often . . . too often, about the night that man, M— F—, said to me, "I can't remember the last time I spent three hours with someone who was less interested in me," and then I got hit on the head with the rusted pipe. Well there's more to that story than I told you that night, not a lot more, but since you do know when I'm telling the truth and when I'm embellishing (though you would not profess to) I'll fill in.

When he said those words to me we were standing in the hallway of his apartment building (his apartment was upstairs) and after I sort of bumbled around apologizing for a couple of minutes trying to explain myself he tried to kiss me. Kiss me! And I said, out of what I first thought was confusion, but now understand was more like rage, "I'm really a little left behind by the turns this evening has all of a sudden been taking and I'd like to go home."

He said nothing, I left, and, two blocks later got thumped on the head. I got home about one, I think, sleeping out of the question, and the phone rang at two. It was M— F— wanting to tell me that I had made him want to throw out the window everything he thought he knew about women. (You might wonder how I managed to do this, since all I did according to him was talk about myself.)

I ended the conversation as quickly as I could. I'd been crying, and didn't want to discuss that with him. He called a few more times after that, but talked only to my voice mail . . . he always said he'd wait to hear from me, so I thought the best thing to do was to not encourage him. I heard nothing these last two weeks until yesterday when there was a message on my voice mail asking me to return a book he claims he leant me, which, of course, he did not.

This is not a particularly interesting story . . . another crazy *person living alone in the city. I find it mildly interesting that the person who suggested we meet, a woman, is about as exciting and quirky as Wonder Bread, but only mildly. And after L—, M— F—'s craziness seems minor league, and happily, he doesn't know where I live.*

It would be easy to dismiss him as crazy and stupid and wrong on all counts, but the thing that haunts me, the thing that I can't let go of, the thing I was thinking about when I got hit that night was the kernel of truth in what he said . . . which is that I don't ask questions . . . I've been trained not to by my father, by my mother, my teachers, and by all the men in my life who wanted so badly to hide. And you want to hide too sometimes . . . we all do, but not always. And when you ask me to come out of hiding it is such a strong and fine thing. . . .

I feel right now how I feel when I'm in front of a room of four hundred people, and someone has asked me a question and it has somehow launched me into some long complicated and well told story and I get to the winding up place, where I'm going to bring it all ever-so-elegantly back around to the question and I have no idea what the question was . . . no idea, as I look out into the crowd, even who asked it.

What are you saying, Pam?

Just this:

I love knowing you. And I want to know everything you want me to know, even if I don't have the sense, or the strength, or the grace to ask.

I described our conversations to H— the other day in a manner that I thought you would appreciate, because I know you know this feeling well. I said our talks held in them a similar pleasure as when I am walking in a vast and varied foreign country with no map or guidebook, only intuition and faith, and I am feeling it, breathing it, taking in every bit I can of that strange landscape, when I round a corner and everything has gone suddenly familiar, and I don't know if it's a function of time spent or knowledge or karma or past lives, but when it's happened to me, as it has in Georgetown, and the Ardeche, Alaska certainly, even the Amazon, almost instantly at the ranch, I understand it for the gift it is. And that's how it is when I talk to you, the undiscovered and the familiar bumping against each other like the knees of teenagers at the Pizza Hut after the basketball game, unchaperoned for the very first time . . . (Oh my God she's off again)

I'll miss the Fed Ex man if I don't stop now.

P—

B—

It's Tuesday night . . . late, I don't know what time, and I'm supposed to be writing the lecture I have to give tomorrow. I'm feeling more and more like I'm in solitary confinement here, though I've made some connections with some wonderful people, and my students are pretty good and pretty smart. It's the no phone/no mail thing, and the scarred walls and the horrible bathroom with its horrible shower curtain that's hung in such a tight circle I can't take a shower without the slimy thing draping itself all over me like something out of a bad film.

*Last night I stayed off campus in a crazy lady's gypsy cara-
van. Her name is E— and she gave me a pair of earrings she
made, a moon in one ear and a star in the other. She grows
flowers and garlic in her garden for money and is in love with
a Polynesian man named H— who drinks too much beer and
then gets mad. He left last night, before I got there for dinner,
so we had several hours of good woman talk, she and her daughter, T—, and I, and then I went to sleep in the caravan in
their yard, with lots of candles burning and Robbie Robertson
playing on the stereo. Candles and music were just the ticket
after sleeping in this sterile place all these days. H— was home
by morning, everything patched up by the time I left for school.
She's got a horse she wants me to ride that she says is real
skittish. There's a beach you can ride to from her house that's
covered, at low tide, with every color of sea glass. I'm gonna
ride out there Thursday afternoon if I can take the time away.*

*This is the wrong place for me to be now. I just want to be
still for a little while. To sit on the porch and just lean up
against you . . . or like we did on the Divide, remember, I just
want to lean up against you and have you tell me things. . . .*

*Hello again. It's Thursday night now, about midnight and
there's a party going on next door with some kind of loud awful
music playing, so I'm gonna finish this letter and then go back
to E—'s and crawl in the caravan again. I snuck away for a
few hours this afternoon and rode her crazy horse, Apollo, about
ten miles down the beach. We had a little rodeo action more
than once but he wasn't really committed to getting me off his*

back. There's something pure magic about galloping a horse next to the ocean . . . even when what I am most of all is scared. I didn't quite make it to glass beach, but on the way back I wrote the beginning of a poem about not making it, so I guess that's almost as good as getting there. I was nearly there, I think, but there was a big log across the thin strip of beach there was. The tide was coming in and when I asked Apollo to go in the water he did a pretty firm 180 on me with a couple of crow hops, and sometimes it feels like wisdom to just let the horse win. E— and I are gonna get up at five tomorrow morning and hike into glass beach. I've got to be back here to teach at nine.

E— told me the story today of how she and H— got together. They'd been high school sweethearts, had lost touch for 25 years when she started dreaming about him. In her dreams he was always sick or dying, in some kind of terrible trouble that in the dream she couldn't prevent. Her husband had walked out on her after eighteen years of marriage. She was trying to man-age her farm on her own. But the dreams continued so she called a number she had long ago that belonged to his sister. She was more than a little surprised when it was H— who picked up the phone. The first thing he told her was that he was a junkie, that he'd spent most of his life in prison, the rest in Vietnam. She asked him if he looked the same and he said yes but his hair was silver. The silver fox was his nickname in prison. They made plans to see each other later that year. When she went to southern California they had less than 24 hours together to see what was between them. She was raising two girls, was concerned for their safety if she brought him around.

He said he'd come help her with the farm, and if she wanted, he'd trade beer for drugs. She spent two months in the deciding, unlike her, she said, not to know right away. She was driving home one night from work, thinking she'd go mad with indecision, begging the universe to give her a sign. A silver fox sprinted across the road in front of her vehicle. She called H— and told him to come the next day.

You can see why I like her. You can see why she found me. I met H— today, finally, and his magic is evident. They have a yard full of red and white gladiolus now, taller, even, than you.

P—

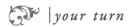 | *your turn*

To write a letter well, Houston writes them in love. Choosing people you love to address in your journal will go a long way in propelling your entry writing. Here are three tacks to take that resemble Houston's strategies:

1. In Houston's first letter, the writing is meticulously detailed about the relationship between the horse and the rider, and it is philosophical about this relationship as well. The undercurrent is, of course, that perhaps as a couple in love, she and her correspondee are experiencing some of the relationship qualities of a horse and rider. To try your hand at a similar-style journal entry, think of someone you care deeply about now or have cared for in the past (a junior high or high school love, for instance), a person you believe will enjoy hearing from you in the form of a long letter.

As Houston does, begin as if you are merely continuing a conversation. Houston writes, "It is, in fact called 'breaking horses,' " as if the recipient of the letter had just said something or was listening to something she was already saying. Imagine what your correspondee might have said and begin by answering it or imagine what you were saying and continue. Then write two or three anecdotes about how you know what you just wrote to be true. See where this takes you. When you feel finished, try for an ending like Houston's where she lists details and images from her Texas trip, saying in each moment that she sees her love for her correspondee. What images and details will you list? How do you see your love in them?

2. This time try your hand at writing a journal entry in the form of a letter to someone who would be interested in an odd encounter you've had, recently or in the past. Write telling your correspondee about the encounter, in detail, and then write explaining why you are doing so.

Houston says, in the second letter, "I love knowing you." Go ahead and make an affirmative statement about your correspondee or your relationship to him or her. After you make this statement, think about what else you want your correspondee to know, and write some more.

3. Make a commitment to writing twice in one day—two segments of a letter to someone you believe knows you well. The first time, write during a self-imposed break from being busy. If you are driving home from work, pull over and park for ten to twenty minutes and write. Or write during a break from work. If you can, skip taking a phone

call and write during the time you would have been on the phone. Write to someone who you feel has your best interests at heart, who wants you to succeed in life and understands the pitfalls. Write about what might be keeping you from finding a still place inside at the moment. For the second segment, write before going to bed. Write about something someone told you during the day and what it makes you feel about life.

Fenton Johnson's journaling example

Nonfiction writer Fenton Johnson proclaims a journal never provided the necessary reality check or the sense of an audience before which and for which he performs. "Letters were and are a different matter," according to Fenton:

Beginning earlier than my twenties—since I was old enough to write—I've used letters to record the passing events and impressions of my life. For me they present the advantage of engaging a known audience (my correspondent). The history my reader and I share lifts me out of myself; it reminds me that what I am about is not just expression but also communication. I write with intimacy because I know I am writing a friend; but I am bound by the discipline of letters to order my thoughts so that my audience may comprehend what I am trying to say.

Excerpts from letters, which were written during my partner's illness from AIDS or after his death in Paris in October 1990 later became passages in larger, longer works. The letter of 14 January

1991 became the concluding paragraph of a chapter of my second novel, *Scissors, Paper, Rock*. The other letters became part of a memoir, *Geography of the Heart*.

As I write I am in motion—500 m.p.h. at 35,000 feet, a place and state of being I find conducive to writing; something about the stale, recycled air and the dog biscuit lunch, combined with that ineffable sense of being suspended in between, neither here nor there, the place where anything might happen even if it usually doesn't. I write in a Palmer longhand much deteriorated from the penmanship classes of my Catholic grade-school days; letters which, on returning home, I enter into my laptop, print out, and mail to one friend or another, saving a copy for my own files. Passages from those letters frequently form the germ of a story, an essay, even a book.

Returning from the journey to France during which my partner and lover died, I wrote his eulogy, an unbearably hard thing to do, in the form of a letter. In a paroxysm of epistolary love, Barbara Kingsolver and I wrote each other monthly for several years, five- and six-page, single-spaced tomes that covered everything from politics to literature to a mock marriage proposal which I accepted, and which I like to think remains in force in some polygamous, parallel universe. (Beware, however, of epistolary romances. A year later I carried on a similar, almost daily correspondence with a man who lived all of fifteen miles away, only to have the real relationship collapse the moment we had to communicate without cut-and-paste. Even so, at the risk of being thought crass I note that the romance served my writer's ends: It gave me the opportunity to record for a known audience my moment-by-moment experience of the world.)

In this difficult, overcrowded, complicated, troubled time, it seems to me that simply to endure without descending into easy bitterness, to sustain some kind of hope and faith for one's peers and for those who follow—this is an achievement, an ongoing act of courage whose magnitude we too often take for granted. Journals or letters—these are means (may they endure and multiply) for declaring the significance of the small thing; a record of the ordinary acts of life and love which bind us one to another, and which are our only true source of hope.

Following are three journal entries by Johnson in the form of letters:

14 January 1991
Dear B.,
. . . Grief is like any wound—there is some terrible pleasure in it. It's better to need that wound, that terrible pleasure than to have nothing at all. If love fulfills itself in companionship, grief fulfills itself in solitude, for we grieve finally and necessarily less for the dead than for our living selves, our aloneness in our survival, our inescapable invitation to the dance.

12 December 1990
Dear J. & J.,
. . . I was reading through Samuel Pepys' diaries—he lived in London at the time of the plague—the "Black Death" of 1655 . . . What's remarkable about his diaries is his attitude toward death—his supposition that it may come at any time, and is handed out by a capricious and not necessarily merciful God (an attitude much closer to the ancient Greeks than to

that of contemporary Americans). Pepys is never far from an acknowledgment of the mystery of things, and the ways in which all things, but most especially his health and prosperity, are dependent on the will of God. These days we would mock that as naive at best, and at worst an embodiment of Calvinism's so convenient dictum that material success is the best evidence of God's blessing. But in reading Pepys' diary his forthright and trustworthy voice comes through, and one understands the depth and sincerity of his belief in his absolute dependence on the whims of circumstance.

. . . I keep searching for some letter from [my partner], some piece of writing that says, "I know you'll be reading this after I'm gone, and I want to say to you that I'm still here." I go into his room again and again searching for that letter and it's never there. I know of course that it wouldn't make any difference, I know what I know and I know, or at least suspect, the ways in which he is with me now and will always be with me; and yet, and yet. I write this not by way of being maudlin but of bowing down before the mysterious fates, which allowed us the three-and-one-quarter years together that we needed to say everything that needed to be said, once, and we said it, once, and once it was said that was the end of it all. For virtually the entire relationship, he said to me, "I'm so lucky," again and again. A week before he died, I turned to him in the courtyard of the Picasso Museum, under a dusk-deep sapphire sky and said, "I'm so lucky." And it was as if the time allotted to him to teach this lesson, the time allotted to me to learn it, had been consumed, and there was nothing left but the facts of things to play out. At the risk of being sententious I say: Think on these things, and

what they mean to you. All relationships are mortal, it's just that most of the time we're too "well-wadded with stupidity," as George Eliot would have it, or needing a gun pointed to our heads, as Flannery O'Connor would have it, and we avoid thinking about it. And then it happens, and it's over. There's no door more unquestionable, more unanswering than death.

7 December 1989
Dear N.,

. . . Today is the memorial service for a good friend of mine . . . he died, of course, of the Big A. We'll all gather in some all-purpose room somewhere and there under the fluorescent lights we'll mark the occasion of his passing, with little ceremony or ritual.

There's something about seeing, actually viewing a corpse that brings home the fact of death, I think; "closure," a Californian would say, which is ironic, since it's been more or less Californians who have eliminated funerals from the cultural scene. . . . It will seem odd, the bunch of us gathered without our friend himself, dead as he might be, as the focus of our gathering. One believes and hopes that his presence will be there, and after all there are plenty (including my friend, from what I knew of him) who would find the presence of a body gruesome. And yet to me this underscores the necessary and vital fact of death in life. One could make the argument that in some measure our lack of respect for the living earth—for its resources, for our place among them, for life itself—has its roots in our lack of respect for the dead, since it is from among the dead that we rise up.

Some time ago, on a late-autumn visit [to Kentucky], I took a car into the hills, looking for the gravestone of one of the men killed in the sporadic wars between the hill families and the state police. I went to Holy Cross Church, where I'd never before set foot, no matter that it is ten miles from where I grew up.

Holy Cross is the loveliest of a series of lovely, early-nineteenth-century churches that Catholic emigrants from Maryland built in this small valley. The church sits on a slight knoll, raising it above the surrounding fields—site of the first Catholic church east of the Appalachians, built in 1787, according to the historical marker; the present church dates from 1825.

Unlike most American churches (but like many European village churches), Holy Cross Church sits in the midst of its graveyard. It's built of red brick, in the simplest of cruciforms, decorated only by curving lines of brick laid into the masonry facade. These curves are echoed in the curving lines of the wooden bell tower, painted white and topped with green shingles. The effect is that of an American primitive architecture, created by people who had no formal architectural training but who were first-rate craftsmen and who, in their simple way, took time and patience to create something beautiful and in harmony with its surroundings—the brick was fired in Kentucky, from the same kind of clay that underlies this churchyard. Looking at the church, it's easy to see how it's of a piece with the land on which it sits.

The churchyard was filled with black walnut trees, which on that early winter afternoon raised bare branching silhouettes against the sky. Spongy black walnut shells were scattered among the tombstones, leaching purple-black stains onto their limestone and granite. From the churchyard I looked down to the hamlet's single intersection (the "holy cross"), where limestone rocks unearthed by the thrifty gravediggers have been used to build retaining walls and a shrine for a plaster statue of the Virgin.

As I stood in the churchyard amid the graves of families whose names I'd never even heard, in the graying winter light, with the black branching limbs of the walnuts and the gray-bleached bones of an abandoned farmhouse silhouetted against the steel blue of the surrounding hills—a sense of sadness, of loss pervaded everything.

Years later, sitting in the Sinai Memorial Chapel in San Francisco, listening to an elderly tenor sing a pure, haunting kaddish, I thought about this: What happens to all that energy of grief when people have no way to give it voice? Where does it go?

✍ |*your turn*

You can use the strategies Fenton Johnson's entries adopt to write more letter entries in your journal. The following three exercises show you how to model your entries on his as well as how to use his thoughts as a diving board for your own entries.

1. In a journal entry, use the letter form to write your way to a question. Think of someone you like to think with, someone who has viewpoints similar to yours. Write to the person about something important going on in your day— a memorial service like Johnson went to; an appointment with a doctor, client or boss; a date or a party. Describe the scene of this event in detail.

Next start a new paragraph and describe something you experienced earlier in your life that on the surface may not be of the same nature. Write in detail about that event.

When you are done, take a deep breath, and raise a question: What has writing about these two scenes, past and present, caused you to reflect upon?

2. Imagine someone writing a letter to you that you will discover after he or she is gone. What would the person share with you? What would the person describe? What would she want you to remember about her and the time she shared with you? Create a journal entry in which you write the letter in that person's voice, telling you what he or she would like you to know and remember.

3. Take a difficult subject—love, death, abandonment, violation, failure or weakness, for instance. Write one short paragraph about your subject addressed to someone you think will understand. Start the paragraph by using a metaphor. Johnson writes "Grief is like any wound." What can you say: Love is like a bowl of soup that is too hot to put into your mouth, even by spoonfuls, so you keep looking forward to it. Death makes the deceased's life a cameo performance. If you have ever felt abandoned you know what to measure your own fortitude against.

Write your metaphor and continue writing for a bit.

Shawn Wong's journaling example

Fiction writer and poet Shawn Wong says:

My journal is my letters. When I was eighteen I started thinking about becoming a writer, but as an undergraduate student and later as a graduate student in creative writing, I didn't really have a career as a writer so I wrote letters, sometimes as many as five or six letters a day. In looking back at the thousands of pages of letters, I realize those letters were how I practiced my writing. In my letters, twenty-plus years ago, I recalled conversations I had during the day and wrote dialogue, looked for teaching jobs, sent manuscripts out, described myself and my writing, wrote to other writer friends and was sentimental and flirtatious with girlfriends. The letters to writers are particularly interesting because many of them were in the same early stages of their careers. When I was a student at Berkeley, I remember thinking how it was strange that professors never assigned work by living authors, let alone Asian American authors and other contemporary American minority authors. So I set out to find them on my own. The community of writers that I found and worked with now reads like the table of contents from any American multicultural anthology of literature: Ishmael Reed, Frank Chin, Lawson Inada, Al Young, Mei-mei Berssenbrugge, Leslie Silko, Victor Hernandez Cruz, Jessica Hagedorn, Ntozake Shange, Rudolfo Anaya, Hisaye Yamamoto, Quincy Troupe and dozens of others. We started literary organizations, publishing companies, journals and magazines, read each others' works and wrote letters. Those letters serve as a valuable record of our beginnings as writers.

As I started publishing and having a career as a writer and a professor, I wrote fewer letters and I worked out my fiction less and less in my letters. For the past ten years I have used the phone more, the fax machine and now e-mail. With the exception of letters sent on the Internet, I still save copies of my letters. I'm afraid my letters aren't as interesting, or romantic, or sentimental, or humorous as they were twenty years ago. For the most part, they're now instructive and informational. I can afford to dial long distance now, so I do. As a professor at the University of Washington for the past twelve years, I probably write more memos than personal letters (the verse form that begins with the stanzas "TO: / FROM: / RE:"). The various drafts of my fiction and other writings are my journals. I still keep meticulous notes on my whereabouts, meetings, travels. For example, on April 9, 1994, I was in Bellagio, Italy, and had a lunch of chicken ravioli soup, duck with a tangerine glaze, cornbread, baked tomatoes with parmesan and raspberry cake for dessert.

I was once audited by the IRS, and I found that I could reconstruct my life from all these separate pieces of information. I remember the IRS auditor began his investigation as to whether my writing was a profession or a hobby by asking in a mocking tone of voice, "It says here on your return that you are a writer. So, how many books have you written?" At that time I had written and published three, so I answered his question and handed him the books. He was so surprised that he stuttered and then asked permission to photocopy the covers of the books. As I went about my task of documenting the fiscal activity of my profession, I realized that in looking over my records I had to control my tendency to tell him stories rather than justify expenses.

The following journal entry by Shawn Wong is a letter he wrote to someone he dated while living on the ocean in Marin County. He wrote from New York City after he attended the publication party for his first book. He later revised this letter and inserted it into his first novel, *Homebase*.

April 2, 1974/New York City
Dear Rhonda,

. . . I've been staying up late nights still trying to catch up on the time, eating dinner around nine, then going out nights to check things out. Then home again to work on a novel I've been writing for a couple of years now. I've rewritten the damn thing five times, each time it gets longer; now I think I've got the thing licked. I'm convinced I got the last chapter in hand. The story about a young Chinese American kid who suffers from dreams, dreams about his father, grandfather, great grandfather. And in the end, Rhonda, he's split up with his Indian girl friend 'cause he ain't no Indian . . . he knows who he is now. He's down at the lagoon by the ocean waiting for a train, that old night train that used to steam down out of the Sierras to come and pick up the Chinese workers wherever they are. It finds homeless men, picks them up, runs through America like a ghost.

That's what I'm doing now, waiting for that train to come and pick me up. I'm thinking about that picture of my father taken when he was twenty-eight years old. He's sitting in that wooden lawn chair. He's relaxed and smiling as though he's celebrating something. So that's why I'm down here at this small boat dock. I brought down a wooden folding chair and a wooden crate for a table from my uncle's house. I went back to the house for a cup of coffee and some magazines. It will be four more years before I'm twenty-eight, but I'm celebrating my twenty-eighth birthday today. I feel good about this day and how it got warmer as it got closer to noon. I read my magazines with my sunglasses on because it was one of those rare sunny days out here on the lagoon. But it's not just my birthday I'm celebrating. I'm waiting for that night train to come around the bend up there where the beach turns to the north. My waiting is a celebration. I've become a patient man like my father.

🐟 | *your turn*

1. Using Wong's letter to Rhonda as an example, write a journal entry that is a letter about something you are struggling with at the moment—a business deal, a difficult person, a career or school decision or a way to say something to someone, for instance.

First decide on the struggle you will describe and address. Next decide on someone to address your words to, someone who lives in a different geographical area than you do. Then write the person a letter that describes in detail what you are struggling with and what you think will happen. Finally, switch topics—tell this person how you are feeling now as you are writing and tell why and what you think this feeling says about you.

2. Sometime soon, do this same exercise again writing about the same struggle to a different person on a different day. You will see how the last part of the letter that addresses how you are feeling changes because you are talking to

someone else who shares a different kind of time and experience with you.

3. Now choose a different struggle and address it to one of the two people you have already written to or to someone else. You will see how the letter works as a meditation for you to come to some understanding, insight or renewal.

Write to people you care about or to those you wish knew you better, and you will certainly write entries in which you come to know more about yourself!

CHAPTER SEVEN

fishing for stories

F iction writers often get their ideas for stories from real-
life settings, dreams and incidents. In this chapter, I
will share journal entries by three fiction writers. They each
tell us how the thoughts and observations they put in their
journals became part of their published stories. Even if you
never intend to write fiction from your journal entries, emu-
lating these authors can be fun and rewarding for your journal keeping. Imagine yourself making your life a story, novel
or film, and in the imagining, write some meaningful journal entries.

Robert Hellenga's journaling example

Novelist Robert Hellenga wrote:

I began keeping a journal on Ash Wednesday 1979 with the following portentous announcement to myself: "Time for amendment of
life." The only requirement I set myself was that I enter something
every single day. Well, I have neither amended my life, nor have I

entered something in my journal every single day. I have written a lot of stuff, however, and am presently on notebook no. 71. That's a lot of notebooks to keep track of, so when I finish one, I make an index that will help me locate sketches, scenes, descriptions, accounts of what I've eaten, etc.

In keeping a journal I've been very much influenced by Dorothea Brande's *Becoming a Writer*, and I have tried to follow her advice, which I shall now pass on: Write regularly (so you don't have to waste time and energy reinventing your schedule every day); write a lot (to develop writing muscles—cf. training for a race or practicing for a recital); write without stopping (so your inner critic doesn't have a chance to intervene).

Following are journal entries Hellenga made during two different trips to Italy:

[Journal Entry #1: Thursday 28 May 1981. Florence. This is my first time in Italy. I'm living with an Italian family and struggling to survive in an intensive language class.]
Giovedi
28 Maggio
Ufficio postale
What a difference a day makes. Yesterday (Tuesday) I was ready to pack it up. The pressure at the school is terrific, and not only from the 4 teachers but also from the other students. Felt really homesick—partly because I went home right after class—& home is a long way from downtown. House seemed empty. Lonely. Wed. Took laundry. Lavasecco first—near bus stop (dry cleaners). Left pants & shirts there. Got directions to

a lavanderia. *Left underwear in nylon bag. This was near the Piazza Cure—glad I discovered it—shops, restaurants, etc. Very near home.*

Decided to find a groc. store to shop in regularly. Went back to Via Faentina—but everything was closed there. Had to go back to Piazza Cure. Bought some olives, artichokes hearts, salame toscano. *(I already had some cheese at home). Bottle of wine. £1000.*

The Raugeis not home. I studied for a while & then ate at kitchen table. The Raugeis came home just as I finished. Sat & talked for quite a while. Sig.a R. sewed up my new sweater.

❧

People. In morning—met a Swedish girl at bus stop. Very nice. Going to a different language school (Michelangelo).

Swiss girl whom I met first day. (This girl is staying with Sig.a R's sister). A bit snippy. Smart looking but not attractive. We spoke German. When I learned that she knew English, I said: "You prob. speak Eng. better than I speak German." She: "I hope so."

Rode home w. her on bus Tue. night:

Thurs.

Grey day.
no Swedish girl.
Swiss girl.

Much better day in school. More relaxed. I wonder if they have the psychology of the whole experience doped out. Are they delib. easing up, or are we just getting used to it???

I did better this morning. I think I'll be able to overcome the others soon, though the Swiss girl [Erika] is very strong willed.

Bernard, Erika, & I each missed 3 on a test. Sara went over each mistake. Anna Maria missed 8, and Elmer (from Austria) 14. He may be the first to crack.

Pranzo. Wed. Vitello con funghi.

Thur. Roast rabbit.—coniglio.

first rate. excellent sauce.

Ravioli for first course. OK. I gave Anna Marie a taste & she complained about too much salt.—made some snide remarks about Americans.

She tosses our salad. Interesting. puts a little salt & pepper in a big spoon w. vinegar—Stirs it around & then puts it on the salad.

An idea for a story is emerging. X goes to Florence. Has a relationship with someone who doesn't speak English. THE IDEA OF THE STORY IS HIS ATTEMPT TO EXPLAIN SOMETHING VERY IMPORTANT (his daughter's death?) IN ITALIAN & CAN'T EXPRESS HIMSELF. Lots of possibilities here. LANGUAGE is power.

1. Teacher-student. The teachers can intimidate the students because they know the language.—Even a young girl teacher can tyrannize over me.

2. Between equals, however, there are other factors. The Swiss girl who lives near me has the upper hand because she has forced me to speak English—to acknowledge that her English is better than my German. But, I have gained the upper hand over Elmer by establishing German as the language we use when Italian fails. (I am sure that his English is better than my German.)

3. With the Raugeis I have (in a sense) the upper hand because I know (!) two languages & they only know one.

4. W. Swedish girl. She got upper hand a little by getting us to speak English. But I can get the advantage back by insisting that we speak Italian.

No doubt there are more possibilities.

❦

[Journal Entry #2: Friday 26 June 1981. Rome. This is the last day of my first trip to Italy. I did a little shopping, went on a bus tour, and mistook a Frenchman for an Italian.]

Friday

More shopping

Oil can. cannol tubes—then bought more.

7 ties. For Ed, Brady, etc.

I did a lot of debating about this, but now I'm glad I bought them.

Olive oil—2 liters.

grappa.

Tour of Castelli di Roma. Rode around in the bus for quite a while [to pick up people at other hotels]. An old man complained: "How many more hotel we stop. Hotel hotel hotel. No see nothing."

I think there was a mix up somewhere. We went to one place & then another—a long drive—to join [the actual tour] bus.

Drove around.

After first stop I decided to sit with an Italian who turned out to be French—no communication!

Wine at Frascatti. I cd. easily have drunk too much. Met an English couple—very nice—hell of an accent. from Manchester—daughter works for embassy in Rome.

⁓⧉⁓

[Journal entry #3: Saturday 9 September 1989. Florence. Walking around the neighborhood where I lived with my family for a year in 1982–83 I encounter a Frenchwoman who doesn't know any English or Italian.]

sabbato

Stazione SMN, 10:07

Didn't get up till 12:30!

Pranzo. Spaghetti w tomato & basil. Similar to "summer pasta." (They said I cd. put cheese on it if I liked. Obviously you don't usually.)

Left over arista *[pork roast].* Salame toscano. *Veal scaloppini. Salad. wine & water.*

Studied most of the afternoon.

Went out about 6:00

Chilly!

*Bus in station. I was going to go to Fiesole & walk to Settignano—*senza carta. *But no. 10 bus came first. Went to Settignano. Walked down to see Sig.a Marchetti. Fancy new gate— electric. TV viewer—speaker. It was after 7:00 & I was a little reluctant—But I pushed the buzzer. She was delighted to see me. We had a nice talk—some grapefruit juice. She told me* *about Paola—married & divorced. a baby. She helps a lot w. the baby. Alessandra studying in Colorado. Am. boyfriend who speaks Italian.*

She was going to Paola's. Drove me down to bus stop (#14). Took bus into town—Got off by Post Office near our old apartment.

Walked around old neighborhood. Rush of emotion at the arch. had to do w. family associations. So much time there. Feeling of its being a special place. (a Chinese rest. on corner of Borgo Pinti.)

Street very narrow & dark. Walked past no. 31

Walked around past Trattoria Maremmana. Still pretty reasonable. Menu turistico *for 15.000 to 23.000. Had a pizza at Pizzeria e Trattoria del Angolo. £5000 & £3000 for a large glass of beer! £1500 coperto. £9500 & tip. Not cheap.*

Sat next to two Americans. young guy w. funny 2-layer haircut. Girl not esp. attractive.

He: this is where the Renaissance really reached its peak Brunelleschi's dome.

She: Where?

He: the duomo.

He didn't want her to order a glass of beer. She was going to order milk but couldn't think of the word. Latta?

Two striking women. One w. streaks of blond hair in brown.

One w. huge tits that she stuck out when she put her leather coat on.

What do I want? not to have heads turn & to have people say, there goes the famous travel writer. To function inconspicu-

*ously in Italy. To chat w. the man at the bar—cash register.
To discuss the menu w. waiter.*

French woman in Pz. Ambrogio, asking for acqua. Acqua
Arno. *She wanted the river. Couldn't speak Eng. or It.
Couldn't see map without glasses.*

Walked home along Arno. No lights after Ponte _____.
*About an hour from Santa Croce. Not a specially pleasant
walk. Finished* Falling in Place. *Didn't sleep well but not too
bad.*

❧

*[Journal Entry #4: Monday 11 September 1989. Florence. I
start to write about my first trip to Italy in 1981.]*

*Brit. Institute—overlooking Arno
lunedi 11 settembre*

*I'd recovered from acute homesickness [back in 1981]—esp.
as the end drew near & I knew I was going to make it. But I
was glad to put Florence behind me. Went to Rome. Stayed in
a hotel. Not especially nice, but I felt* free. libero. *To come &
go as I pleased. Rome was big & breezy—like Chicago. Big
wide streets—Big open spaces.*

*Confident—in restaurants—in the hotel. I was speaking
Italian.*

*Bus trip on 3rd day. Via Appia from hotel. Wound up
sitting next to some Americans. Wanted to speak Italian on my
last day. Finally moved to seat next to a distinguished man
who'd kept to himself. Looked a little funny to me—but . . .*

He turned out to be French. couldn't speak a word of Italian.

I said: "Je parle un peu français."

He perked up a little.

It was true. I can read French & when I was in France I cd. sort of speak it. But Italian had driven it all out of my head. The only thing I cd. say in French was "Je parle un peux français"! That was it. Absolutely!

He must have thought I was very strange!!!

※

[Journal entry #5: Thursday 21 September 1989. Florence. I spend too much money on a leather jacket.]

giovedì 21 sett. 89

[Casa] Ciammarughi

The jacket. After class went right to Raspini to pick it up— (to bank this morning.) Nervous. so much money—took off money belt. No one grimaced. On hanger—folded in a sack.

Didn't want anyone to see it! Didn't want to wear it!

Didn't want anyone to see me carrying the Raspini sack either!

went to bar—sandwich: Rustico: prosciutto crudo e salsa di carciofi. *Not all that good.*

Bus home. Snuck sack into my room before going in to say hi to Sig. e Sig.a

Tried coat on. Hung it in closet & hid other coat in suitcase; Raspini sack in suitcase too.

You cd. do quite a lot with this. Maybe write about "Traveler vs Tourist." Sometimes I want to be a tourist—

Buying the coat is a tourist thing to do—reveals a fundamental split.

Cf. reading Dick Francis instead of Nat. Ginzburg—can't even read her in English.

⁓ЭᏨᏋ~

[Journal Entry #6: Tuesday 26 September 1989. Florence. A short story starts to come together.]
Martedi 26 sett. 89
[Casa] Cipriani 9:06
*Idea for a story:

Just a quick sketch: A man wants to be bilingual. After his wife's death he returns to Florence, where he spent a year w. his family.

Living w. a family
Not very comfortable.

Maybe in a room by himself—because language school can't find a family for a man his age. (much easier to place young girls)

Learns things about himself: he's really hoping for romance. Looking at the girls, etc. women on the bus. Thinks if he can master the language he'll have a better chance.

Finally the opportunity presents itself: wandering around old neighborhood Santa Croce. Eats a pizza. on way back to his room—beautiful blond woman—no longer young—not a kid—fashionably dressed, but not in a frightening hands-off way. Suitcase of sorts.

Wants to find the Arno. (what exactly does she say? Acqua. Seems to be calling for acqua.)

Doesn't speak English or Italian.

Protagonist has become pretty proficient in the language. She's French.

He says: "Je peux parler un peu de français." (Title of story: "I Can Speak a Little French")

But then that's all he can say! She looks up expectantly. Tears of relief spring to her eyes—a warm welcoming smile. Starts to speak in French. Protagonist can't understand a word. And he can't come up with anything in French except the phrase: "Je peux parler un peu de français." He's trapped in that phrase. When he repeats it, she smiles and looks expectantly again.

He manages to point her in the direction of the Arno—Lets her go.

It all happened so fast. Took him by surprise. If he'd had a chance to think . . . He cd. have taken her to his room, and then . . .

You didn't need to know French or Italian or English . . .

But couldn't imagine . . .

NB: something more could happen. He cd. follow her. something cd. in fact develop.

or he cd. see her again.

They cd. have a little fling—going out to dinner—unable to speak to each other.

This might in fact be an interesting problem to set your protagonist.

Maybe: if she writes things out he can read them.—or maybe you should just work on them getting along without communicating.

—in contrast to his strong desire to communicate in Italian. At end: "I can speak a little French. Not much, but enough to get by!"

❦

One way to get started: He gets a letter from his daughter in France saying she's found a job and won't be coming [to Italy] after all. This cd. touch off a change from feeling on top of things to the bottom dropping out, i.e., the realization of how lonely he is—and how much he wants to hold someone in his arms.

All the defenses he's been building up fall apart.

Prospect of spending Thanksgiving alone (or at the Am. church, which wasn't quite the same thing—but almost)

—or maybe Christmas

spending Christmas with the French woman—His heart is so full of memories, stuff he wants to tell her—to show her— the apartment on Borgo Pinti—He'd been living right in the center then—the centro storico. *Now he had a room way out in the Novoli—upper left hand corner of the map—if you had the right map—otherwise it might not be there at all.*

Maybe taking a course in Enology—to fill up the time.

His writing project? discrepancy between the renaissance in the visual arts and the other developments political, economic, historical.

(You could do some interesting stuff with the daughter being in France—w. French—preparing for the French woman. Acqua Arno)

Also: sending American postcards to various friends acquain-

tances actually—saying that he was in Florence. But he doesn't hear anything—People who'd been glad to send their children to Chicago for a month at a time—friends of his daughter.

He'd written to them using the tu *form—saying how much he'd like to see them again and perhaps their families too. But nothing.*

He'd been careful w. money—saving up for a big splurge when his daughter came.

Gets involved w. the French woman.

Spends the money on a suede coat.

that he's embarrassed to wear.

From Raspini.

Wears it in his room.

Afraid it's too big.

Goes back.

asks for a brush (ostensible motif)

possibility of exchanging it.

No problem

But no smaller size.

Girl tells him that for a morbida *jacket the line should be down over the shoulder—She touches him to show exactly where. it's just where the line falls. He feels better.*

Christmas dinner w. French woman.

*He thinks he'll burst—he has so much to say. *Imp. development. His Italian is at the point where he can sit down w. one or two people (Italians) and talk about anything—religion, philosophy, story of art, literature, family, love.—his experiences in Italy. (This was where he'd left off before.)*

But the prob. was getting one or two people to sit down and talk to you.

He's older than the students.

You can't just start talking about love & philosophy to the person sitting next to you on the bus. (What was more likely to happen wd. be that someone would turn to him & say something out of context. He'd be taken by surprise—wouldn't know what the person was saying—& then the person wd point to his or her wrist & say "time pleez" & he'd show him (or her) his watch—pulling up his sleeve.

VIP theme: TALK VS SILENCE (w. French woman)

Protagonist setting so much stock on talk—in speaking— Then the big surprise comes from a woman he can't talk to. A woman who offers herself to him (modestly)—& whose offer he almost turns down because she can't speak Italian—because they can't talk to each other.

(She really needs help w. her suitcase, which is very heavy.)

OK: what do they do? How does he communicate to her that he wants to see her again? At the hotel on the Lungarno? (when she sees the river she gets reoriented.)

All this time learning Italian, and now this! Je peux parler un peu de français.

"Doman" "demain"

Maybe he remembers a few more French phrases:
Dans le fond des forêts votre image me suit.

On ne me suit merne pas sortir en hiver.

and one of the first phrases every student (male) figures out:
Voulez-vous couchez avec moi.

(Of course one wouldn't use the 'vous' form!)

fishing for stories | 149

Maybe he remembers these at the hotel. Desperately wants to see her again. Can't talk!

When he entered her he had to bite his lip to keep from crying. (Thinking earlier that he might never make love to a woman again! a real possibility!)

This is such a great gift.

Sees her off at the station.

That night: puts on his new suede jacket. Goes downtown. To tell the truth, he'd been afraid that everyone wd. stare at him. even follow him around.

But nobody noticed. He was invisible. Takes a bus—rides to end of line—cf. when he was a child riding the buses and street cars in Chicago.

An invisible presence traversing the city—like Browning's _____ . Il padrone della città. *Watching over the city—so far from home.*

If someone had asked him, he wd. have said, "I speak a little French. Not much, but enough to get by."

But there was no one to ask.

Hellenga has written that these entries are:

. . . linked by themes and experiences that have shaped a lot of my fiction: Italy itself, the challenge of living in another language, the meaning of "home," etc. They are also linked by the fact that in 1989 I began to write about things that had happened in 1981, and by the fact that on each trip I (1) had a brief encounter with a French person with whom I couldn't communicate, and (2) spent too much money on a jacket. The last journal entry I've included incorporates these experiences into a sketch that eventually (several drafts later) became a short story: "I Speak a Little French" (*Crazyhorse* 43, Winter 1992). I include here a brief excerpt from this story—an encounter with a French woman that grew out of two seemingly insignificant encounters recorded in my journal:

I was about to order another glass of wine when I noticed a young woman crossing the piazza dragging the largest suitcase I'd ever seen. The suitcase had wheels on it so that you could pull it down long airport corridors, but the wheels were too small for the rough paving bricks of the piazza and the suitcase kept tipping over, like a large dog that keeps flopping itself down. She wasn't able to go twenty feet without the suitcase falling, and it was so big and heavy she had trouble setting it upright again. I stepped out from under the arc to get a better look, and when she saw me, in the light of the piazza, she cried out: "*Acqua, acqua.*"

I shrugged my shoulders. After all, there were two bars in the piazza, in addition to the *bettola* [wine shop]. We were in the center of a modern city, not in the middle of the desert.

"*Acqua, acqua.*"

I could hear the tears in her voice.

"*Acqua Arno,*" she said, and it dawned on me that she was looking for the river.

"Right down the via Verdi," I said, in Italian, pointing to the street.

The suitcase tipped over again and this time she left it. "*Acqua, acqua,*" she repeated.

"*Parla italiano?*" I asked, helping her right the suitcase.

"*Acqua, acqua.*"

"English?"

"*Je suis française.*"

"Ah," I said. "*Non parla italiano? o inglese?*"

"*Je suis française,*" she repeated. "*Je suis française.*"

I'd had two years of French in college and said the first thing that popped into my head: "*Je peux parler un peu de français.*"

"*Dieu merci.*" A look of relief rose to her face. "*Je cherche l'Arno, s'il vous plait. . . .*" She kept going, but too fast for me to follow. Quite naturally she expected more, but unfortunately there was no more. To her rapid questions I could make only a single response: "*Je peux parler un peu de français,*" which I kept repeating, hoping that something would click. But nothing clicked. I was imprisoned in a single phrase. What had looked like an open door was a *trompe l'oeil.*

"*Acqua Arno?*" This time it was a tentative question. She had given up. She was a damsel in distress, and I was her knight errant; but without the sword of language I couldn't come to her rescue, so I pointed her, once again, down the via Verdi towards the river—*acqua Arno*—and watched as she crossed the piazza. She reached the post office; the enormous suitcase teetered, tottered, and fell over again. She struggled to set it on its wheels, and then she disappeared around the corner and was gone.

Je peux parler un peu de français. It was ridiculous. It was maddening. *Je peux parler un peu de français.* It didn't occur to me at the time that if I'd gone on in French, in school, instead of switching to Italian, I'd probably be in Paris instead of Florence, or that if she had spoken Italian, she wouldn't be in the middle of the piazza asking for *acqua Arno*. No, all I could think of was that my whole life had been leading up to this point, and I'd studied the wrong language.

🐟 | *your turn*

Write regularly, Hellenga passes on as advice; write a lot and write without stopping. Certainly journal keeping is a natural for attaining those goals. You can follow Hellenga's advice and his example with this three-stage exercise:

1. Make a journal entry every day for a week, or at least once a week for four or so weeks, in which you recount a day, including lots of its mundane details—what you wore, shopped for, ate, how much things cost, the locations of new services you looked for and found. Then, amidst the detail in each of these entries, write about an encounter with a new person, place or object. Include names, conversations and descriptions.

2. After making entries every day for at least a week or once in a while over four weeks, write about a story idea that you could generate from the doings and encounters you'd written about. Outline the story, its protagonist, what he or she wants and what gets in the way.

3. In yet another journal entry, write about what you think the most important part of the story is or what question it raises for you to examine.

Remember, each time you do a part of this exercise, write without stopping. Don't torture yourself over what you are going to say. Just keep writing and find out what you are saying.

Robin Hemley's journaling example

In the following journal entry by fiction writer Robin Hemley, you can see how writers' dreams generate story ideas and plots:

5:00 a.m. 8/25/92

Dreamed I wrote a story based on my relationship with AJ. Free spirit who drives trucks and import cars from one location to another. Stops in town where I live. He's sort of my alterego, makes everything look simple. Always relaxed. People are attracted to him, his open personality. We wind up at a country bar listening to the music of a country star like Tanya Tucker, but her name is something like Swish Swander or Samantha Swan. At one point, he takes out some breath mints and she's singing her way through the audience. He says jokingly that he'll give her a mint if she sings one of her songs, and he names a famous one. She stops at the table and soon she and AJ are talking. She's someone AJ and I might make fun of, but I can't believe a famous star has sat down with us. She and AJ eventually go off together and I'm left to fend for myself. But then he reappears to give me a lift home. He's just given the

woman a ride to her hotel and he's back. And we're friends
again, and he tells me to relax.

- *Base everything on AJ from how he got his name to Sulfur*
  Springs.
- *The country bar is called "Gator's Bar and Boogie."*
- *Set story is Charlotte.*
- *Line dancing*
- *Then I realize I'm someone we might make fun of.*

Mr. Hemley wrote at length about how this dream did,
in fact, form the basis of a story once he made some changes
and introduced some new elements:

My friend AJ grew up in Sulfur Springs, Indiana (I've always loved
that name), but we knew each other at Indiana University in the
late 1970s. AJ is the original free spirit, or at least that's how I
remember him from college. AJ was one of those people who
seemed so open to knowledge and experience that people flocked
to him, someone who always seemed on the verge of discoveries.
The other characteristics that come to mind when thinking of AJ
include an animated, almost manic intelligence, a generous spirit
and above all, a whimsical, unpredictable nature. He was also one
of my most loyal friends, staying in touch with me over the years—
not like clockwork, but unexpectedly calling or appearing when I
didn't expect him. For a time, whenever I visited Chicago (once
or twice a year), I'd run into AJ purely by chance on the street—
this happened three or four times—and AJ didn't live in Chicago
either. He visited the city almost as infrequently as I. In a way, I
thought of AJ as an alter ego.

AJ, by the way, is his real name. Not A period J period. "A" and "J" are his father's initials, but for some reason his mother wanted to give him his father's initials but not his full name.

And AJ had, for a time, the perfect job for a questing free spirit such as himself. For years, he delivered cars and trucks across country to various dealerships and individuals. Once he took me on a wild ride in a railroad truck across northern Indiana, and he'd always send me strange artifacts from his travels across country or accounts of the odd tourist attractions and people he'd come across.

The night I dreamed about AJ, I wrote down the dream in my journal. The dream, strange as it was, immediately suggested a story to me, partly because of the strong demarcation between my personality and AJ's. Obviously, the situation seemed a little skeletal and inscrutable (as dreams often are), but I figured I could work with it, and in any case, I'm often drawn to making incredible scenes seem credible. My wheels were turning as soon as I wrote down the dream, and I plotted the notes to myself below the dream.

I *did* base the story on AJ, though I transformed him somewhat, exaggerating him, making him even more of a prankster than I remember, and I exaggerated the personality traits of the character based on me, making him more harried and neurotic than I am (though that hardly seems possible). I also hinted that he was unhappy in his marriage and that the narrator's wife disliked AJ. My real wife, when she read the story, told me that when AJ read this story I was to tell him that she didn't dislike him. I hasten to add that I'm quite happy in my marriage.

As much as I liked the name "Sulfur Springs," I had to leave it out finally. I didn't want this to be the real AJ, but someone modeled on him. And my initial enthusiasm for the name "Gator Bar and Boogie," evaporated. I did, however, set the story in Charlotte, North Carolina, where I lived at the time, a place I had some antipathy towards, which came out quite strongly in the finished story. Line dancing also figured prominently in the story, as did that line that followed in my journal, the character realization that "*I'm* someone we might make fun of."

Wanting to stay in some ways true to the spirit of the dream, I decided to set the story in a country bar in Charlotte, with the main action occurring more or less as it did in the dream, with some crucial adjustments. Line dancing was in full swing around this time, and I'd never seen line dancing in person, so I enlisted two friends, and under the guise of research we went to a cavernous country bar on one of the main thoroughfares in Charlotte, a tawdry strip called Independence Boulevard. I took notes (of course), on the terrible band that was playing, on the race signs on the wall, the woman selling roses from table to table, the struggling, half-drunk line dancers. I even took notes on the conversations around me and included some of what was said that night in the mouths of my characters.

Here's how the story, titled "Independence Boulevard," which was published orginally in a magazine called, of all things, *Boulevard* (Fall 1994) opens:

> LD's in town, or maybe he's not. Maybe he's calling me from
> Nebraska and just pretending he's in some phone booth in
> a convenience store parking lot near the coliseum. His voice
> sounds like LD's: a hairtrigger laugh inside him, a little high,
> a little hyper. He says, "You want to play?"

"I'll kick your butt," I say.

"I'll whup your ass," he replies, our little ritual.

"You near the old coliseum or the new one?"

He laughs. "I don't know. It looks like something that McDonald's used to package Big Macs in."

"That's the old coliseum," I say. "Out on Independence. You want directions to the house?"

There's a pause. "Why don't you come meet me?"

He doesn't like to come over because he thinks Mary Elizabeth doesn't like him. It's not that. It's just that women are either insanely attracted to LD or repelled by him. There's no in-between. When Mary Elizabeth and I were living together before we got married, LD came over once and insisted on sweeping the kitchen floor. LD can be helpful like that, but Mary Elizabeth was suspicious. She called me at work and asked me if he was safe. Sure, LD's harmless, I said, but he's given her the creeps ever since.

I haven't heard from LD in three years, and I'd almost thought he'd forgotten about me, or given up on me, but being LD's friend is like belonging to the Mafia. One of these days, you're going to get a call, and you won't be able to pretend it's for somebody else. If you're LD's friend, you're stuck for life.

LD's real name is LD, with no periods in between the letters. He was born in Valparaiso, Indiana. His mother didn't want to name him after his father, Lester Dean Conroe, because she thought he was a jerk, but Lester was a big man in town and she wanted to give her son the advantage of being known as Lester's son. So she named him LD. Of course, in the outside world, people don't know who Lester Dean Conroe is, and they think LD stands for something. Like Learning Deficient. It's not that I don't like hanging out with LD. I've known him since college. I'm just not the same person I was fifteen years ago. But LD is. I've matured. I don't like scenes. . . .

As I said, the story is an exaggeration of our personalities. I hope AJ and I aren't quite as childish in real life. We've never done that "whup your butt . . . kick your ass" exchange or anything like it, but it seemed to fit the mood of the story.

LD and the narrator, Kevin, meet at a shady convenience store near the coliseum, where LD pulls a prank on the narrator, centering on a pay phone and some drug-dealing kids. Then LD plays another prank on Kevin, and finally they wind up at a country bar along Independence Boulevard—a mixture of the one in my dream and the one I researched, with my imagination thrown in for good measure. By this time, Kevin, already in a questioning state over his life with Mary Elizabeth, and unbalanced by LD's sudden appearance and prank-playing, starts to question LD's choice of bars in an irritable and bitter way. The singer on stage, a Croatian country-and-western singer named Laurel Dove, has been belting out her tunes to a zombielike crowd who'd rather line dance to canned music, and she's been trying futilely to engage her audience in some friendly stage banter.

"Why did you bring me here?" I ask LD over the noise.
"What?" he yells back.
    "Why did you bring me here?"

LD shrugs. I look at Laurel Dove prancing around, her hair flowing behind her. I wonder what's up with LD. This is the kind of place we would have made fun of ten years ago, but LD looks like he's really into the music, tapping his stubby little fingers on his Lone Star Beer coaster. What's with this Laurel Dove? She's the kind of person we would have made fun of ten years ago.

"You know, Kevin," LD yells suddenly. "You've changed."

"What do you mean?" I ask, warily.

"You've matured. I mean that in a good way. The well of your experience seems deeper."

I almost laugh at that one. LD can be corny sometimes when he's trying to sound wise.

"How can you tell? We've only been together for an hour."

"I can tell," he says wisely and goes back to his beer and the song Laurel Dove is singing.

When Laurel Dove finishes, she yells out, "How many of you . . .?" and stops midsentence. "Hey, y'all out there? Any survivors?" She scans the audience with a hand in front of her eyes. "Oh, fuck this," she says, and walks offstage. For a moment, no one reacts, and then her band members slowly unburden themselves of their instruments and follow her. Then the place fills up again with canned country music, and almost everyone jumps up from their tables and rushes to the dance floor.

LD buys a rose from the rose woman.

"What's that for?" I ask.

"You never know when a rose is going to come in handy," he says, and laughs.

"Give me a break," I tell him.

Presently, Laurel Dove emerges from behind the stage and walks toward the bar. She sits down on one of the stools and the bartender brings her a longneck. She takes it and heads our way.

She stops right in front of our table as though she's on a string that LD's pulling. LD hands her the rose and she takes it and smiles. She sits on his lap, puts her arm around his neck and gives him a kiss. Her hair surrounds them like a curtain.

I've got a buzz. Time has slowed and I'm in that frame of mind where almost anything is acceptable. My head's cocked and my mouth is slightly open and saliva's gathering in the corner for a drool. My voice is a croak, and I'm not sure whether I'm talking or thinking, but a voice in me says, "Yeah, I guess this is truly happening." A woman with hair down to her butt has stepped off the stage, ordered a beer, then made a beeline for our table. She's sat on LD's lap and the two of them are making out. Things like this happen to LD.

I wonder what Mary Elizabeth would think of this. I'd say, "You have to admit. He's got to have something."

While they're making out, I study the place. There's a cactus theme on the walls. My skin feels tingly, like I'm being pricked. I have a cactus in my yard, a big overgrown one that's taking over and choked out some daffodils that Mary Elizabeth planted. If you've ever been pricked by a cactus, you know it's hard to see the little quivers. You just bite them out and swallow, because they're so small. I guess maybe they're still stuck in me, but on the inside where I don't have nerves.

Then I think I'm the kind of person we would have made fun of ten years ago, and this depresses the hell out of me.

Laurel Dove scoots off of LD's lap and LD gives a little laugh. His face is smudged with stage makeup.

"Kevin," he says, "I'd like you to meet my wife, Mara Dovnic, a.k.a. Laurel Dove." Then he bursts out laughing and Laurel Dove nods her head at me. "We met in Nashville. I'm her manager, too."

She gives him an adoring look. "LD keeps me sane." She glances out at the dance floor, gives the line dancers a death-ray look, and turns back. "I've never met anyone like him, have you?"

"No," I say, a bit dazed.

The story doesn't end there, of course. The narrator, angered by this final prank of LD's, asks to be driven home, and the story finishes back at the convenience store where it started. The narrator, in a somewhat altered state from the evening's events, commits, somewhat inadvertently, a convenience-store robbery, turning the tables on the shocked LD, and putting him in a vulnerable position for once. Sounds crazy, I know, but so do a lot of stories and novels in synopsis. As a writer, my job is to make it all seem believable within the context of the story, just as in my dream all the crazy actions seemed credible as they were taking place.

You might notice that I've changed a lot from the original dream I recorded in my journal. In the dream, AJ drove the country singer home and then returned, and we were friends again. In the story,

LD drives Kevin home, and the tension has only intensified by the end of the story. In my journal entry, Laurel Dove was Swish Swander or Samantha Swan, a famous country-and-western singer, but I knew that a real star wouldn't be appearing in such a place. Maybe a has-been or a pseudostar like Laurel Dove. I can't tell you exactly why I made her Croatian, except that I have a good friend who's Croatian, another writer, and maybe this was a subtle tribute to him. Or maybe it was just a quirky detail I liked. Of course, a breath mint didn't seem like much of an offering, maybe even an insult to someone like Laurel Dove who's just been ignored off stage—a rose seemed more appropriate—something that I'd set up earlier in the story and something that I'd seen being sold at the real country bar I visited.

You'll also notice that that original realization I noted in my journal, already somewhat in character—I'm someone we would have made fun of ten years ago—fit into the final story, and became one of the prime despairing epiphanies of my main character, Kevin. I feel the need to emphasize at this point that, although I wrote this thought down in my journal after the dream, it both was and wasn't how I was feeling personally at the time. As a writer, I was already thinking in terms of shaping this dream into a story (not something I do with every journal entry, mind you), and so I was thinking in terms of my character's thought processes. Of course, there was obviously some emotional resonance to me in my own life, and to say otherwise would be disingenuous.

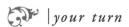 |*your turn*

Once you focus on writing what you remember of your dreams, you will find yourself remembering more and more of your dreams. It is good journal-keeping practice to write as many entries about your dreams as you can.

1. Taking after Hemley, write one or more journal entries that recount dreams you've had in as much detail as you can manage. This would be a good place to use the repetition exercise from chapter two; repeating "This is a dream about" will help you gather the details you need.

2. After you've written several entries that vividly recount some dreams, review the entries. Hatch a story idea from one or more of the dreams you recounted.

3. Next, write an entry that describes where the story takes place and what goes on in the setting you have chosen, who is in the story and what each person's dilemmas are. Think of and write about the ways in which the characters are autobiographical.

4. Then take a trait from one of the characters and give it to the character whom you think closely resembles you. Write about what you think will happen to this character now that he or she has this trait.

Steven Winn's journaling example

Writer Steven Winn recorded this entry in his journal:

August 22—Story idea this morning in bed outdoors, a story called "The Skylight." It begins with the father seeing the skylight like some water blister on the roof from far off in the orchard. Later the analogy of the house to a child's space toy, a rough sort of graft on an old house.

It comes out that the father never liked living in that old house anyway. He has all daughters except for this son—and at first getting the son out of the new house seemed to get him a new daughter—the son's wife. But recently the son has seemed more prominent. He notes the stitch of love in his son's brow, like some tribal decoration.

He wrote about this entry:

How clearly I recall that August morning, and how strange my recording of it in my journal now seems—how specific yet sketchy, prescient and blind.

I did in fact write a short story called "The Skylight," later published in *The Indiana Review* (Vol. 9, No. 1), and it conforms to the situation roughly envisioned here. The protagonist, a farmer in arid eastern Washington, has one son and a number of daughters. His complicated feelings for his son are worked out, as I sensed they would be, in terms of their adjacent houses. In the older house, once occupied by the father and now owned by the son, the son makes various improvements—including a bedroom skylight. The father, having built a new house next door, watches the once dreary old house transformed before his eyes.

But I was "wrong" as often as I was "right" in this entry. The story does begin with the father seeing the skylight from afar, but the water blister image occurs much later in the narrative. Another image that gave the story its first substance for me—the "stitch of love in his son's brow, like some tribal decoration"—disappeared entirely in the writing. And the third, the notion of the house as "a child's space toy, a rough sort of graft on an old house," turned completely opaque and inert. I cannot recapture what I saw, or thought I saw, as I lay staring at a Marin County sky that morning.

"The Skylight" was a visitation, an idea that arrived pretty reliably whole to me. The plot was still to be discovered, as were many other folds and shadows. But the story's life was rooted in the almost physical deliverance of the images, even if the water blister was the only one to survive.

The primacy of the images is the reason, I think (without thinking of it at the time), that I recorded where I was when the idea came—"in bed outdoors." The open-air sleeping arrangement became part of the story's spontaneous gestation. Many of my journal entries are made with a breathless, superstitious haste, often when waking at night or early in the morning. My journal is a phantom catcher. Giving each entry a date and sometimes a setting is a way of trying to tighten the web, strengthen the net.

In this case, I was house-sitting for a Fairfax, California, couple I didn't know very well. Shy of declining their offer to use the mattress on a deck outside the bedroom, I slept outdoors. When I awoke, a tiny silver jet was crossing the sky, trailing an extravagant white plume. And there, in that silent blue morning, was "The Skylight." I got up from the dewy mattress and found the spiral notebook that goes wherever I do.

The detail of the airplane I didn't need to record, for whatever reason. But I remember it now, a sense memory that is as vivid as the water blister. A journal entry preserves an event—this time, the birth of more writing to come—in telegraphic form. Rereading old entries reconstitutes the cryptic jottings into fully fleshed memories. The airplane and cool mattress, though unrecorded, were indelible parts of that August 22 event.

The blister was the divining image of "The Skylight," as it turned out. Water pressed against a translucent membrane was somehow bound up with the swelling audacity of the son's home improvements—of which the skylight was only the most visible to the daunted father. What I didn't know, or knew only subliminally, was that water would figure importantly throughout the story. The climax of "The Skylight" involves a rush of water into a basement; another scene occurs with a long, brown tongue of water lolling between two characters as they converse over an irrigation ditch.

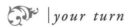 |*your turn*

Steven's journal entry/story idea is the result of sleeping in a new place, one with an unusual feature, a mattress on a deck outside the bedroom. You can help yourself come up with new thoughts for your journal by making sure you "visit" new places from time to time, in this case, places to sleep and perchance to dream.

1. Take a nap in an unusual place—your backyard, on a porch, in the living room or in someone else's room. Promise yourself that when you wake up you will write in your journal about the first thing you see. Write down the name of what you are visually focusing on when you wake up, and then write a metaphor that will demonstrate how you are experiencing what you are describing.

For instance, Winn calls the skylight a water blister. Emulate his ability with metaphor. What does the couch look like where you are—or California poppies or the gas grill or the posters on the wall? As in chapter two, make as many metaphors as you can to offer new experiences of this object.

2. Pick one of the metaphors and decide what person from your life would see the world this way and what his or her emotional state would be. Write about this.

3. Think about a struggle this person would be involved in with others. Write about it. Think about what difficulties he or she would have with people or projects. Write some more.

You can journal from daily experience or from the recollections of dreams. Doing so you'll write the details of the memory and be able to spin some new stories from them, either as more journal entries or as writing for other projects.

PART THREE

add-ons

ten more strategies to use for making journal entries

N ow that you have seen how poets, fiction writers and nonfiction writers keep journals, and you have practiced using some of their strategies, you know firsthand that strategies are a way to get your words on paper and mine your experience for insight. You have experienced how adopting a good "entry strategy," using details that appeal to the five senses, and using metaphor, anaphora and simile and metonymy can help you keep a journal that is rich in insight. Coupling creative strategy with good use of the writing craft, prevents you from writing passages that bore you with generalities or clichés. You find yourself achieving insight and fresh observation without self-consciously digging for it by writing in circles. Additionally, you are less tempted to write what you think you are supposed to write, rather than what you have inside. You are keeping a journal you love, rather than one that puzzles you or feels like a chore. You want to write and write and write! Therefore, in this chapter I share ten more strategies I have used to write entries, as well as advice on how to keep generating new strategy ideas for yourself.

more tried-and-true journal-entry strategies

record the weather, inside and out

Reginald Gibbons has a passage about weather in his novel *Sweetbitter* that stirs me:

> The weather was gathering, threatening rain. A thunderstorm had been building, far off to the west, and now it was going to fill the quiet night with its threats. A sizzling bolt of lightning burst out sideways above them, searing its thick knotted length on the dark sky for a long instant like an engorged vein on the very arm of God. She was blinking up where the flash had been. The immense darkness of the woods around them had turned in the moment of the bolt into a frightening innumerableness of detail, and in that lit instant every leaf and twig, every thread of their clothes and hair on their heads, was counted and recorded. Then came the blasting thunder, pushing through their bodies as if they were nothing, and beyond them echoing away over half the world.

Gibbons has written about jotting notes in his journal

about the rainstorm that later turned up in his novel. He calls this kind of entry a "marker buoy" thrown into the waters to remind him to go back and search the depths.

Concentrating at least once a month on describing weather could yield strong writing in your journal as well as provide "marker buoys" of the emotional weather in your life over a period of time.

Take the time every once in a while when you are making a journal entry to describe the weather you observe at the moment of your writing. Is it day or night? What is gathering or dispersed? Notice the quality of the air—is it stirred up, clear, still, foggy? Notice the moisture in the air—is it humid or dry? Notice clouds and their shapes, the absence or presence of stars, the moon and the sun. Notice the sounds the wind is causing or the way birds react in this weather. Are sounds muffled or sharpened in this weather you are describing? What is the temperature, and how do you respond to it? How do trees look in the weather you are observing? Now, name an element or force that enters this scene similar to the lightning that makes Gibbons's characters concentrate on an infinity of detail. After you select and name the element or force, make a metaphor to describe it in the way Gibbons's does when he says the lightning is the engorged vein of God. Let the metaphor you come up with spin your writing in a new direction just as Gibbons's metaphor lets the very presence of infinity into the moment. If you say the blast of a foghorn in the night is like a dying animal's last moans, it will affect the writing one way; if you say the blast of a foghorn in the night is like the notes your younger brother pushed out when he was first learning to play the tuba, the writing will probably go another way. See what happens when you do this!

write a "things I learned today" list

The late poet William Stafford from Oregon published a poem that was a broad-ranging list of things he learned, supposedly on the day he was writing. He included things he observed by paying attention to what others generally don't take the time to see, such as on which side ants pass each other. He learned things from the newspaper, such as what topics famous people were speaking about. He learned things from doing, such as how to unstick a door. And he learned things about himself by noticing personal preferences. Take some time occasionally to write an entry entitled "Things I Learned Today" or "This Week" or "This Month" and go on in detail, including information you've learned by personal observation and personal experience as well as facts and theories you've read or heard in the media and learned through books, classes and people. Consult your inner self for insights that have occurred to you. Include information that has come to you in dreams. And be sure your list has variation from really important to small and seemingly insignificant pieces of information like Uncle Harry was married once before he married Aunt Sally, the no. 24 bus runs from where I live to the rec center where I want to go to regularly work out, Sara Lee is making a new frozen coffee crumb cake that reminds me of one my mother used to make. The variety of importance, the variety of methods of learning the information and the detail with which you write about things will help you create a very interesting journal entry. After you have written all the things you can think of about learning, take your lead from Stafford—he writes "If I should ever die, I would like it to be. . . ." End your entry with a sentence that starts, "If I ever," and finish it with something that will happen to you,,, i.e., "If I ever breathe again," or "If I ever say 'I love you." Writing a sentence that begins this way automatically pulls all the other details and information onto a deeper plane of meaning.

use prompts

Many writers who teach suggest students begin writing from a prompt that centers and focuses their writing without prescribing what must be written. Ron Carlson suggests beginning writing by thinking of a song or piece of music and stating, "The last time I heard _____, I was _____." Fill in a specific piece of music and then begin writing about what you were doing, where you were, who was there and what was going on. Let the occasion you create be your guide.

Here are some more prompts to use when you sit down to make a journal entry and don't know quite what you want to write about:

- "The last thing I ate before I sat down to write this entry was _____ and the next thing I might eat is _____ . This is because . . .

- "When I look up from my page, the first thing I see is _____ . I like/don't like this because . . .
- "Here are five things I should not have put in the trash and this is why . . .
- "Here are five things I ought to put in the trash and here is why . . .
- "If I could describe the place where I am writing to a set designer for a movie, here is what I would say . . .
- "When I go to the White House for dinner, I always wear my _____ and take along my _____ . That way . . .
- "When the nightly news director put a caption under my picture to identify me to the people, the words were _____ . This is what had happened . . .
- Turn on the radio for twenty seconds. Write about what you heard.
- Ask a friend to make a list of five more prompts you might use. Ask that the prompts be written on individual pieces of paper. Open the prompt only when you are ready to use it so you don't think about what you will write ahead of time. That way you will get fresh ideas on the page and not censor some interesting thoughts or descriptions!

play the alphabet game

Make the alphabet your friend. Challenge yourself to put down your thoughts entry by entry with titles that start with each letter of the alphabet for twenty-six contiguous entries.

Or challenge yourself to start each entry itself for twenty-six days with words that begin with the alphabet's letters in order. Or write twenty-six meditations, one on each letter of the alphabet. Or create an entry in which each sentence starts with a word that begins with consecutive letters of the alphabet.

create persona entries

In a famous fiction-writing exercise by novelist John Gardner, the writer must describe a lake from the point of view of a man who has just committed a murder, but the writer can't say this has happened. Then the writer must describe the same lake from the point of view of a man who has just fallen in love without saying that this is what is going on for him. This exercise establishes the way a speaker's internal world colors what he or she sees in the outer world.

For fun in journal entries, think of someone or something that would have an interesting stance on the world—your pet, your telephone, your refrigerator, the cereal box you left open in the morning, one of the Halloween costumes you wore as a child, your steering wheel, someone you know has suffered a joyous or a difficult situation. Write as if you are that person or thing addressing you in a letter. Let the persona you are creating tell about their environment or their day without naming who or what they are!

play the "and then" game

In beginning drama classes, acting teachers sometimes introduce a game in which students stand in a circle and take turns telling a story sentence by sentence. The only rule is that after the first person states a sentence, each person begins the next sentence and part of the story with, "And then. . . ." What happens next does not have to be plausible, just interesting. Try writing in your journal this way. You will find yourself coming upon amusing ideas, and you will begin to see opportunities for storytelling.

take another lesson from the declaration of independence

You can copy Thomas Jefferson's technique of repetition to gather details that will ultimately allow you to write down a philosophy of life. In fact, write "Philosophy of Life" as a title for a journal entry and use Jefferson's phrase, "I hold this truth to be self-evident," as the one you will repeat. Write it down and then write whatever occurs to you to write next. When you have come to an end, write "I hold this truth to be self-evident" again. Let this sentence become either the first phrase of every line or a phrase that weaves through your entry every once in a while. Keep writing. When you feel you are finished, read what you have written in light of the title. I am sure you will have evoked a philosophy of life.

write one-sided telephone conversations

I am always entertained by listening to people on the phone. When an actor in a play talks on the phone, I am convinced there is someone on the other end of the line even though

I know he is talking without a telephone partner. I once asked an actor friend how they handled that, and he told me the actor has to imagine that someone is talking and fit his pacing and expressions to the ghost talker on the other end of the line. In movies, both parties are shown on a split screen or by edits from one phone to another. These conversations are much less mysterious to be sure! A good journal-writing idea is to imagine yourself on stage talking on the phone. The audience has only your words, posture, expressions and gestures to understand what the other party is saying and to what you are responding. Furthermore, perhaps the conversation has already started when the curtain goes up, and the audience is coming in on the middle of something. Go ahead and write a monologue—your side of a lengthy conversation with someone. Imagine what the person is saying and have yourself responding, gesturing, pacing, sitting, slumping and fidgeting accordingly. Here are some possible ways to open:

- Yes, it really happened the way I said it did!
- You can't mean you don't believe me!
- I just do. I don't know why, but I just do.
- And then I was around the corner and . . .
- You won't be hearing from me too soon because . . .
- Wouldn't you know that . . .

dispense advice

Nobody wants unsolicited advice, we are told, and giving it won't win you friends, so giving it in a journal entry is a great idea! What else to do with all the ideas we have for others? Choose someone you feel is in need of doing things the way you would do them or have them done—a spouse, child, in-law, parent, teacher, boss, co-worker, neighbor, clerk, business owner, politician, police officer, dog walker, etc. Write this person a letter giving detailed advice and telling why you are doing so. Give as many examples as you can explaining why you know what you are talking about and how you know your advice is effective.

write definitions

If someone asks you to tell what something is or what it means, you usually begin by describing the thing or action. You tell how it looks, sounds, smells, tastes and feels. You tell what it does and what it doesn't do. You tell what people use it for and what it is never used for. You tell what it is like and how it is different from what it is like. You might tell an anecdote that illustrates something about it, or you might give an example from your life as illustration.

Make a point of collecting words that you do not know the meaning of. They are all around us in the form of words that are the actual technical names for things and processes we haven't heard of, foreign words or words we just have not yet learned the meaning of. Write your own definition for these words before you look them up or find out anymore about them. Using the techniques I've listed, you'll create an inventive piece of writing.

In addition, make a point of inventing words for things

that don't have names. A friend of mine shared the word "zorblot," which she and her sister coined to name the piles they began to see filling the space in their recently widowed mother's home. Another friend told me about the word "zenseleeb," which she uses to name the crumbs in the sink after she has washed the dishes and someone has eaten a cookie or sandwich over the sink. Go ahead and start naming things that don't have names yet and write about them. I mean, how did we get words like "heebie-jeebies" and "the willies"?

hints on devising more great journal entry strategies

read, read, read!

Newspapers. What is most noticeable about newspapers? Headlines, columns, pictures and ads. Why not make up some exercises that utilize these aspects of writing? Can you write an ad for something in your life? Why not paste pictures in your journal and write accompanying articles? Write in column form and see if you think differently seeing your words appeal that way. Start entries with headlines as if they were in a newspaper. Try telling your day in terms of headlines. Write an ongoing opinion column for your journal.

Magazines. Feature stories and the way magazines use them to attract readers jump out at anyone browsing the newsstands. What does this suggest as a writing strategy for you in making journal entries? Something about how to spin the story of your day, week, month or situation to make the front page of a certain magazine? Choose magazines you think your life stories and thoughts could appear in. Write your entry as if it were an article in one of those magazines—give it bullet points or sidebars if the magazine you are thinking of does this. Give it the format the magazine likes, e.g., how to, gossipy snippets, interview format.

Books. Make a habit of finding books written in the form of journals. Many exist as both fiction and nonfiction. In addition, read the published letters and journals of famous or interesting people. Make a note of strategies they use in their entries and commit to trying each strategy out at least once. Note in your entry who you are imitating and why.

Poems. Collect poems you like from books, magazines, the Internet and anthologies. Paste one in your journal from time to time, and write a poem or a letter back to the poet, using the strategy and phrasing the poet used in his or her poem. Have fun sounding like the poet whose work you admire!

Stories, TV programs and movies. Watching these can lead to strategies for keeping a journal. Adopt a character or a setting you are intrigued with and write entries from that point of view. Or write entries about what you think happened to the character or setting after the story was over. Or write down your reaction to the stories, your questions and concerns, or your delights and favorite memories.

Greeting cards. Keep cards people send you. Browse

card-shop stock. Create a line of cards of your own. Is it funny or spiritual? Nature-oriented or about people and their idiosyncratic ways? What occasions are they for? From time to time, write the text for some of these cards in your journal and add accompanying pictures or drawings. Create more lines of greeting cards to write.

Cereal boxes and other packages. We read lots of these in our lives. Pay attention to the wording and information on several boxes in your house or on store shelves. Imagine that you are creating packaging for things in your life, and write the blurbs and anecdotes you think people would like to see on whatever box you are stuffing these things into. And remember, the things you are packaging can be impossible to package other than in your fantasies!

listen, listen, listen!

Listening to conversations around you and to the media can yield interesting rhetorical strategies to copy. Here is a list of things I notice when I listen to people and broadcasts:

Clichés. Notice how people use them. Are they conversation openers or do they shut down conversation? Imitate this in your writing. Or make note of the clichés, and use them as jumping-off points for writing meditations. What do the clichés mean if you stop and really pay attention to them?

Excuses. Notice the excuses people offer for their awkwardness, clumsiness, lack of timeliness, inabilities and other characteristics. Use some of these excuses in journal entries. Imagine yourself saying these things about something you don't want to do.

Unfinished sentences. People don't talk in full sentences. Even if they intend to, others often interrupt them before they finish their sentence. Notice this in conversations. Try writing a journal entry in which you don't finish any of your sentences. Either imagine an interrupter or write one in!

Exclamations. You hear people saying these a lot: "Wow!" "My goodness!" "Really!" "What are you, crazy?" "Bite me!" "Unbelievable!" Keep a running list of exclamations and use them in journal writing. Use one as a title and then do a freewrite and see what you have to say. Use one as the phrase for the anaphora technique introduced in chapter two. Write a dialogue in which you are a speaker and the person you are speaking to can only answer you in exclamations. Try this the other way around, too.

Complaining. Isn't there a lot of this around! Pay attention to what people complain about to waitresses, agents at airport gates, grocery-store clerks, teachers and customer-service personnel, as well as each other, especially children to their parents and vice versa. Write down some of your favorites from among those you hear. From time to time, start journal entries with one or more of these complaints. Do a freewrite seeing if you can complain in this way using details of your own experience. It'll be interesting to see what you get off your chest!

Babbling. One thing you'll notice for sure is that most people hate a silence and will fill it with words, words,

words. Note this in the conversations around you. Write some of this word noise down as an entry. Then start a new paragraph and write in caps the word "SILENCE." Start writing again. It will be interesting to notice the difference between the babble and what you say after you scream out for silence and clear space for yourself.

look, look, look!

We are always observing something even if we are not paying full attention to what is in our midst or what we are in the midst of. When you keep a journal, you become more aware of your surroundings, and in becoming more aware, your surroundings can supply you with some writing ideas. You may start with a sense of sight, but the other senses will come into play as well.

Scenes. From time to time, imagine you have just come where you are with a camera. Imagine yourself taking a picture and after it is developed, looking at what you captured. Write about what you notice in your picture, what it is composed of and what it makes you aware of remembering.

Quiet. Sometimes all we see is quiet. This is hard to come by in our noisy, busy world, but we can find it whether in an empty room at night or a park on a rainy day. Go find some quiet. What does quiet look like? Write about what it sounds like, tastes like, smells like and feels like. What are the things that are missing that ensure the quiet? What are the things that are there that ensure the quiet?

Movement. Even in the most still moment, there is movement around us. A tiny circulation of air, a bird darting onto a branch, a fly buzzing. Go somewhere and notice what is moving. Write about all that you see, and try to describe the movements you observe so that each is distinct and has different verbs associated with it.

Commerce. We are very busy buying and selling in this culture. Watch transactions around you in a day. Who is buying what from whom? Describe some of these scenes involving others, then end with a scene involving yourself. How is the scene involving yourself the same and different than the other scenes you observed? What might you conclude from all this buying and selling? Write this in your entry.

Nature. Writing about nature is important to most writers, whether they live in the country or the city. Gardens, parks, trees, birds, dogs, cats and zoo animals end up in their writing. Sometime when you are making a journal entry, list what you can see of nature from where you are writing. What do these bits of nature have to say to you at the moment? Let them speak to you. Frank O'Hara wrote a famous poem entitled "A True Account of Talking to the Sun at Fire Island" in which the sun comes to visit him on Fire Island, waking him up. Let whatever elements of nature you can see have things to tell you, and they will undoubtedly wake you up!

Maintenance. As much as we see buying and selling and

nature in our surroundings, we see maintenance—all the activity of keeping things going, running, repaired. From time to time write a journal entry about something in your life that is being maintained or repaired or is in need of repair. What is wrong with it? What is the actual maintenance or repair required? Who is doing it? How long does it take? Why is it important? Is it noisy or quiet? Expensive or not costly at all? Does it require special tools or materials? Do you know the person or people doing the work? What do they look like while they do it? After you write about the maintenance or repair, create a blessing you might make over the repair or maintenance people, for the process itself or for the object. You might be writing about interpersonal processes as well as about roads, appliances, gardens, lawns, motors, etc.

What I've shared is in no way a complete list of places to look for inspiration in creating strategies for making journal entries; it is only a sample of how I borrow from the world to make myself find open-ended but intriguing ways to start writing. I look for a strategy that is like a game—something with a little twist in it so I can't know the ending before I write myself there.

Now that you have practiced with ideas from professional writers and with ideas I've shown you, I hope you will find yourself wanting to create journal-writing exercises that you definitely want to get started using!

CHAPTER NINE

creating journal-keeping groups and communities

After reading the journal entries of fifteen writers, you may feel like you are part of a journal-keeping community. Many people find dedicated journaling groups very helpful in their process of keeping a private book of writing. Often these groups are writing circles where members sit together and write from prompts, twenty or so minutes for each. Members offer themselves as audiences for the writing if the journal keeper wants to read hers aloud. The groups share perceptions about journaling research findings, and they share information on resources for journal keepers. Some of these groups have professional facilitators and others meet without teachers.

An new extension of the traditional journal-keeping group is made up of the many online Web sites available now. Journaling enthusiasts post journal-writing ideas as well as samples of journal writing. Often these sites encourage participation from those who would like to become part of an online journaling community. In addition, many splendid bibliographies especially for journal keepers appear online. Recently, I typed the key words "journaling for self-discovery" (the subtitle of one of my books) into the Yahoo search engine (www.yahoo.com). A page of sites to explore popped onto my screen, and I followed the links to online bookstores, discussions on journaling and even instruction. Among my favorite online resources were www.wholeheart.com with resources and a newsletter, and The Center for Journal Therapy (www.journaltherapy.com) with information on classes and new software for keeping a journal on your computer. About.com also has a page on journals and journal keeping.

No matter how helpful you find online resources, however, finding the people in your community committed to journaling will enhance not only your journal keeping, but your life. I know a woman who began sharing her journaling experience with a few others, then began teaching journal keeping and facilitating groups; she organized a newsletter to support those keeping journals and ultimately went back to school in a top-notch graduate program in psychology. Other people report that the long-lasting relationships they've maintained with journal groups, who have listened to their writings about deaths, divorces and illnesses, were the most healing avenues in their lives. Having members of a group to write with, to count on for listening and to listen to was instrumental in their recovery and self-growth.

finding a journal-keeping group

If you decide you want to find a group to help you start or continue journaling, look into the various continuing education resources in your community. Look at catalogs for extension programs at local universities and colleges, especially at listings of their writing and self-help offerings. See if any of the offerings focus on keeping a journal— of any kind! You might find people teaching sketchbook, journal keeping for writers, or nature and travel journals. Check with churches, libraries and community centers as well as area bookstores to find out if they host or sponsor journal-keeping groups. Sometimes these are in the form of groups keeping morning pages after the work of Julia Cameron, author of the popular book *The Artist's Way: A Spiritual Path to Higher Creativity*, or support groups for grief, illness, parenting and employment searches. Any class or group that requires keeping a journal is a good place to start because you will be in the company of people who want to take pen to paper and record their observations and perceptions. You can use the strategies you've practiced in this book for helping yourself journal on particular topics as well as on whatever comes to mind.

how do I create my own group?

You may prefer to create your own group of journal keepers. I believe five to eight people is an ideal number. That number fits comfortably in any room or around most tables. With this number of people, it is possible to create trust and respect while facilitating and responding to variety in life occasions. In addition, if one or two members are not able to attend a particular meeting, there will still be a fruitful number of people present.

You might begin finding your groupmates with a "call for interested parties" or article in an organization newsletter asking people to contact you. You might also have some friends or acquaintances from classes you have taken or groups you belong to that you feel would be interested. Send them a copy of the article or ad you write. Don't hesitate to call a group of people together who you feel will work supportively and with commitment. Beware of asking those who know you are asking simply because you think you should to be kind or stay popular or keep from hurting feelings. Your journaling group requires a special place in your life, and just because particular others are important to your life in many ways, it does not mean they are good journal groupmates for you. Sometimes, coming together with people just for journal keeping can facilitate your ability to write deeply because you are not worried about how you feel you must appear in the others' eyes on other occasions.

Explain in a piece of writing (that will appear in the article you write or that you can send to those who respond to your call) some of the benefits of journal keeping. Also clearly state the attitude and goals you have as a journal keeper. You might want to quote from one or more of the writers in this book. Then, explain your idea of how the group will work and how long and how often it will meet.

selecting a meeting place

Think about whether you want your group to meet in a space provided by an institution or corporation or in homes.

I have known groups to use space provided by public libraries, community centers, public schools, colleges and universities, lunch programs, bookstores, corporate and privately owned offices, and coffeehouses. If you want to use a space outside of your home or the homes of others in the group, think about the availability in your community of the kinds of spaces I've listed. Start making calls to see who you must ask and what paperwork you must fill out to secure a location. You might have a day of the month and time to meet already selected so you can secure the space in the hopes that your group will materialize. On the other hand, if you want the group as a whole to decide, it is good to know the options before your first meeting, which you might hold in one of those spaces if it is available.

If you want to meet in homes, decide if you want the group to come to your home each time or whether you would prefer to have a meeting that rotates among the members' homes. Be prepared to discuss the pros and cons of this setup with those who come to the first meeting. Many people like knowing where the meeting will be each time. Others don't mind a rotating place as long as the next place is decided at the end of each meeting. Others don't mind rotating, but don't have the ability to host the meetings at their home. Some people don't want to feel like hosts when they are concentrating on journaling. Others find the intimacy of a home more appealing than a public space for this kind of work and sharing. There is no one answer to what is best for journaling groups, but you can decide what will work best for you as the organizer and for the group to keep meetings happening and highly functional.

getting comfortable with each other and maintaining a commitment to the work

I think people become comfortable with each other in a group most quickly when the group goal is clear and well supported by the agenda, and when the members speak without judgment about people's abilities. Warmth, trust and acceptance are important in a setting in which people are going to write from their personal experience and deepest feelings and perhaps share that writing.

Asking for a simple introduction by each member is an important step in building bonds. The person's name, interest in journaling and reason for wanting to be part of a journal-keeping group are most important to share. It is not necessary always to know a person's occupation and marital status to build the kind of rapport necessary for the journaling group. These particulars will get themselves known before long. What is important is that the group from the very beginning stays focused on its goal of facilitating journal keeping.

Clearly stating the ways in which the group will facilitate the keeping of journals is very important. Encourage members to speak about the way in which a group might help them keep journaling. They might want to address things they've experienced that have not been helpful or wishes they have for this group.

addressing privacy issues

No matter what reasons have brought people to the group and no matter how experienced or inexperienced people are in keeping journals or in working in a journal-keeping group, knowing that what they share in the group does not go out of the group is extremely important. Time must be taken for having the group discuss their fears, needs, requests and delights about the privacy that a good journal-keeping group maintains for its members.

handling feelings

Some of us are demonstrative and some of us are very private about our emotions. Even so, most of us don't like breaking down in tears among others. Some of us have a hard time handling the tears of those around us. Somehow, a group that journals together must be prepared for tears, laughter, anger, joy, exhilaration and feelings of helplessness, and they must know how to accept them. Addressing this in a first meeting can help set the tone for trust and respect. An easy way to open the topic is to acknowledge that there may be times when members require tissues to wipe away tears of pain and of joy. Promise a box will always be available at the group ready to be passed along.

You might want to address how the group can best respond to strong feelings. One way to do this is to ask members to recall and write about a time someone helped them by accepting their feelings. How did this person show acceptance? Each member who wants to can read to the group from this piece of writing. It is likely that no discussion will be needed after this concerning how to best deal with strong feelings. Listening, modeling the taking of deep breaths, gently offering a tissue or a break may be among the best responses because they allow the member to decide how to continue.

A journaling group offers a place to have feelings and experiences heard and accepted and not altered by even helpful responses or advice. It is a place to hear oneself just as a journal is a place to begin to listen to oneself. This is powerful, important and priceless. Sometimes members' tears are their deepest thanks for a rare opportunity.

refreshments or not?

Groups differ on their feelings about combining snacks with their meetings. Some people have simple finger foods and snacks for those who have come from work and need some nourishment because of skipped dinners. Coffee and tea are often mainstays. I think each group has to monitor for themselves their needs concerning refreshments. Is food helping people settle into the group meeting, or is it distracting people from the goals of the group? Is the food easy to get together and serve, or is food becoming a competitive, annoying hassle for those who share the responsibility of providing it? Is food served first, throughout the meeting or at the end of the group's time together? Again, there are no steadfast rules. The group needs to evaluate their needs and how the refreshments are either serving or not serving these needs. Sharing food is an age-old way of building trust, security and connection. Whatever way the group handles refreshments should be in the service of these goals.

the meeting content

Here is a list of questions for you and your group to consider when deciding how to use journal-group time:

Will you write in the group or only outside of the group? Some people prefer to get centered in journaling after spending so much time away from the life of the journal keeper by doing an exercise at the start of the group. Other people would like even more time devoted to writing during the group meetings as a way of keeping up their journals and learning new strategies and prompts for writing. Others want their group time for sharing their entries with trusted listeners so their words, thoughts and feelings come alive outside of the journal pages. Many want some time in each group to discuss and share information about writing, writers and journal keeping.

Group members must decide for themselves how much time will be allocated at each meeting for writing, sharing and discovering resources. Perhaps group members will decide they want to have a different focus at each meeting over a period of months. Journal-keeping meetings do tend to be lengthy—two and a half to three or even four hours is not unusual.

Will you all use a particular book as members of this group? Often groups adopt a book to use and follow in an effort to stay focused and dive more deeply into journal keeping. There are many fine books out there. You might want to select one to use or have a few for the group to choose from if you want to work from one guide at a time for a while. If each member owns a copy of the book, then the group can not only listen to the writing promoted by the book's exercises, but discuss the author's way of approaching journaling.

Will you listen to each other's journal entries and respond? How? My experience with people keeping journals is that they do enjoy sharing some entries with others. In this way, they experience their own thinking, feeling and memories more fully than if they don't share what they have written with others. And people coming together in a group that respects journal writing are eager for the opportunity to talk in authentic voices and be heard.

How we respond to the information and feeling given to us by the journal keeper is very important. Some things make us clap for joy, laugh heartily or grow somber or sad. When a group registers its feelings upon receiving the journal keeper's words, the response is valuable because it reflects and validates the journal keeper's own feelings. It brings the journal keeper from enriching solitude to enriching connection with others and our shared qualities in being human. It is very important that this be accomplished without correction or judgment but with acceptance. Therefore, in listening to shared journal writing, the group's first responsibility is to listen attentively and to reflect without judgment or alteration the ways in which the writing is moving them. The group might say back memorable words and phrases just as they heard them, and they may tell the reader what feelings they are having after hearing the journal entry. If the person sharing has asked for this, the group may contribute ideas on how she might use her journal entry to create other writing on the subject.

Will you have a meeting facilitator or share that load among the members? Depending on the wishes and talents of those in the group, one person might facilitate all meetings or different people may be selected in turn to faciliate individual meetings. The job of the facilitator is to make sure that everyone who wants to read from their journal gets the time to do that, that the response and acceptance for the piece is without judgment or distraction, and that the group has time to write from prompts if writing is scheduled. Sometimes the facilitator is responsible for bringing the prompts, or individuals each bring a prompt, or the group knows the prompts because it has chosen to work from a text. Using prompts in the group is a natural way to start sharing resources. The more places people find writing prompts, the more places everyone in the group knows of to go to for ideas.

Will you share information and resources on journaling? In addition to prompts, there are other resources on journaling and writing from classes and newsletters to books, lectures and Web sites.

As a group, you might want to subscribe to one or more newsletters. You might want to build a lending library of books on journaling that you can circulate amongst members. Your group might want to belong to a writing society that provides information and contacts that foster writing and journal keeping. The International Women's Writing Guild [P.O. Box 810, Gracie Station, New York, New York 10028-0082/(212) 737-7536] and The Center for Journal Therapy [12477 W. Cedar Drive, #102, Lakewood, Colorado 80228/(888) 421-2298] are two such groups.

You might want to allocate time at meetings for news notes and announcements, or you might keep an e-mail, phone and address list so members can send each other information as they get it.

You might also enjoy reading the published journals or letters of others as a group. Perhaps the group can meet occasionally to explore responses to the ways writers, scientists, politicians, adventurers, parents, ill or handicapped, war and crime victims, celebrities and pioneers kept journals.

Will you engage professionals or others of interest from time to time as guests? Sometimes groups decide that they would like some input into their processes or some new ideas or connection to the world of writing and journaling. Sometimes members know of local authors, teachers, therapists or students of writing who are willing to come to one of their meetings and talk with the group about journal keeping. Sometimes the group members contribute money to offer the guest an honorarium. Having a guest once in a while helps a group renew its delight in continuing the journal-keeping process.

Might you want as a group to join in other activities that will help you thrive as journal keepers? Keeping excited and committed is hard sometimes. In addition to inviting speakers to come to the group, the group might want as a whole to attend lectures, readings, festivals and other events that will enrich their journal-keeping experience. Since journal keeping is so related to creative writing and to philosophy, therapy, adventuring, nature observation and religion, there is bound to be a wealth of opportunity nearby for satisfying and inspiring activities. In addition to attending events that get the group out and listening to the notions and experience of people they might admire, the group can also invent activities that they will then journal about. Such activities might include taking a hike or bicycle trip together; camping or attending a cabin retreat; going to a play, dance performance or concert; taking a walking tour, a garden tour or a tour of artists' studios.

how can we build a larger journal-keeping community or influence our community as an outgrowth of journal keeping?

In addition to the self-nurturing events suggested previously, group members can volunteer for community services and build bonds not only to each other and their journals, but to the larger community. Volunteering at centers to help people keep journals is a logical way of extending the journaling process. Your group might want eventually to offer journaling groups in senior care centers, detention centers, or schools and hospitals. Group members might want to act as journal-keeping liasons with professionals who serve these populations.

In addition, group members might want to extend themselves to the community by performing services and keeping journals about the work, whether it is serving hot meals, cleaning up beaches, helping preserve a wetland or taking housebound people outdoors. These journals might make good publication material for the community's newspapers, helping many better understand the needs of specific populations and geography. Once we honor our own authentic voices, we have an urgency about cultivating and responding to the authentic voices of others. In this way, journaling unites people and communities.

Now that you have reached the end of this book, you have written quite a bit in your first journal or continued an established journal-keeping habit by (1) peeking into the journals of professional writers, (2) reading their thoughts on the journaling process, and (3) enhancing your own writing skills and desire for solitude. Perhaps you have already connected with others in a journal-writing group or community or are now about to.

"The passing of time contributes to a refreshing perspective," David Mas Masumoto writes. My hope is that you are refreshed by the freedom of your journal writing, the ease with which you can get going now that you have so many strategies and ideas to use and the feeling of peace after you have had your say. My hope is that meeting like-minded people, both in this book and in your life, has contributed to a sense of well being. Finally, because to love something truly is to pay close attention to it and because the exercises in this book have fostered your ability to do that, my fondest hope for you is that you love the journal you are keeping.

BIBLIOGRAPHY

Published journals and letters that have influenced the writers whose entries are in this book:

Agee, James. *The Collected Short Prose of James Agee*. Ed. by Robert Fitzgerald. London: Calder and Boyars, 1972.

——. *Letters of James Agee to Father Flye*. Boston: Houghton Mifflin, 1971.

Bair, Deirdre. *Samuel Beckett: A Biography*. New York: Summit Books, 1990.

Camus, Albert. *American Journals*. Trans. by Hugh Levick. New York: Marlowe & Co., 1995.

Carroll, Jim. *The Basketball Diaries*. New York: Penguin Books, 1987.

Cheever, John. *The Letters of John Cheever*. Ed. by Benjamin Cheever. London: Cape, 1989.

Coleridge, Samuel Taylor. *Anima Poetae: From the Unpublished Note-Books of Samuel Taylor Coleridge*. Ed. by Ernest Hartley Coleridge. Folcroft, Pa.: Folcroft Library Editions, 1977.

Didion, Joan. *Slouching Towards Bethlehem*. New York: Modern Library, 2000.

Dostoevskaia, Anna Grigor'evna Snitkina. *The Diary of Dostoyevsky's Wife*. Ed. by René Fülöp-Miller and Dr. Fr. Eckstein. Trans. by Madge Pemberton. New York: The Macmillan Company, 1928.

Emerson, Ralph Waldo. *Emerson in His Journals*. Ed. by Joel Porte. Cambridge, Mass.: Belknap Press of Harvard University Press, 1982.

————. *The Heart of Emerson's Journals.* Ed. by Bliss Perry. New York: Dover Publications, 1995.

Fitzgerald, F. Scott. *The Crack-Up.* Ed. by Edmund Wilson. New York: New Directions Pub. Corp., 1993.

Frank, Anne. *The Diary of a Young Girl: The Definitive Edition.* Ed. by Otto H. Frank and Mirjam Pressler. Trans. by Susan Massotty. New York: Doubleday, 1995.

Fraser, Rebecca. *The Brontës: Charlotte Brontë and Her Family.* New York: Crown, 1988.

Gide, André. *The Journals of André Gide.* Ed., trans. by Justin O' Brien. New York: Vintage Books, 1956.

James, Henry. *The Ambassadors.* Ed. by Leon Edel. Boston: Houghton Mifflin, 1960.

Joyce, James. *Letters.* Ed. by Stuart Gilbert. New York: Viking Press, 1957.

O'Connor, Flannery. *The Habit of Being: Letters of Flannery O'Connor.* Ed. by Sally Fitzgerald. New York: Vintage Books, 1980.

————. *Mystery and Manners: Occasional Prose.* Ed. by Sally and Robert Fitzgerald. London: Faber and Faber Ltd., 1972.

Pepys, Samuel. *Pepys' Diary.* Girard, Kan.: Haldeman-Julius Company, 1922.

————. *The Shorter Pepys.* Ed. by Robert Latham. Berkeley: University of California Press, 1985.

Powell, Dawn. *The Diaries of Dawn Powell. 1931–1965.* Ed. by Tim Page. South Royalton, Vermont: Steerfort Press, 1995.

Rainer, Tristine. *The New Diary: How to Use a Journal for Self-Guidance and Expanded Creativity.* Los Angeles: J. P. Tarcher, 1978.

Rilke, Rainer Maria. *Letters on Cézanne.* Ed. by Clara Rilke. Trans. by Joel Agee. New York: Fromm International Pub. Corp., 1985.

———. *Letters to a Young Poet.* Trans. by Joan M. Burnham. Novato, Calif.: New World Library, 2000.

———. *Selected Letters of Rainer Maria Rilke.* Ed. by Harry T. Moore. New York: W.H. Norton & Company, Inc., 1960.

Roethke, Theodore. *Straw for the Fire: From the Notebooks of Theodore Roethke.* Ed. by David Wagoner. Seattle: University of Washington Press, 1980.

Saroyan, William. *The Twin Adventures: The Adventures of William Saroyan, a Diary. The Adventures of Wesley Jackson, a Novel.* New York: Harcourt Brace, 1950.

Sarton, May. *The House by the Sea: A Journal.* New York: Norton, 1977.

Sexton, Anne. *Anne Sexton: A Self-Portrait in Letters.* Ed. by Linda Gray Sexton and Lois Ames. Boston: Houghton Mifflin, 1991.

Thoreau, Henry David. *The Illustrated Walden.* Ed. by J. Lyndon Shanley. Princeton: Princeton University Press, 1973.

Tolstaia, Sof'ia Andreevna. *The Diary of Tolstoy's Wife.* New York: Payson and Clarke Ltd., 1929.

Weil, Simone. *First and Last Notebooks.* Trans. by Richard Rees. London, New York: Oxford University Press, 1970.

———. *The Simone Weil Reader.* Ed. by George A. Panichas. New York: McKay, 1977.

Woolf, Virginia. *To the Lighthouse.* Ed. by Sandra Kemp. London, New York: Routledge, 1994.

Wordsworth, Dorothy and William Wordsworth. *Home at Grasmere: Extracts From the Journals of Dorothy Wordsworth and From the Poems of William Wordsworth.* Ed. by Collett Clark. New York: Viking Press, 1979.

contributors' notes

KATHLEEN ALCALÁ'S books include *Mrs. Vargas and the Dead Naturalists* (stories) and three novels, *Spirits of the Ordinary, The Flower in the Skull* and the recent *Treasures in Heaven*, all set in nineteenth-century Mexico. Ms. Alcalá has received the Pacific Northwest Booksellers Award, the Governor's Writer's Award and the Western States Book Award for Fiction. She cofounded *The Raven Chronicles*, continues as contributing editor and is on the board of *The Seattle Review*.

RON CARLSON is the author of five books of fiction, most recently the story collection *The Hotel Eden*. His novel *The Speed of Light* will be published in Fall 2001. His fiction has twice been noted by *The New York Times* as one of the best books of the year.

ROBERT HELLENGA is the author of the novels *The Sixteen Pleasures* and *The Fall of a Sparrow*, which made the *Los Angeles Times'* list of "Best Fiction of 1998" and *Publisher's Weekly's* "Best '98 Books" list. He has received several Illinois Arts Council Artists' Grants as well as a National Endowment for the Arts Fellowship and the PEN Syndicated Fiction Award. His fiction has appeared in many literary magazines and his nonfiction appeared in *The National Geographic, The New York Times Magazine* and *Sky* among other publications. He is professor of English at Knox College in Galesburg, Illinois.

ROBIN HEMLEY has published five books, including two short story collections (*All You can Eat* and *The Big Ear*), a novel (*The Last Studebaker*), a book on form (*Turning Life Into Fiction*) and a memoir (*Nola: A Memoir of Faith, Art, and Madness*). He is currently at work on a nonfiction book from Farrar, Straus and Giroux about a purported anthropological hoax in the Philippines. He has received the Independent Publishers Book Award, the Governor's Award from the State of Washington, the Nelson Algren Award, two Pushcart Prizes, *Story Magazine's* Humor Award and The George Garrett Award for Fiction. His stories have been read on NPR's "Sound of Writing" and "Selected Shorts." A full professor at Western Washington University, he will spend Spring 2001 as the first Viebranz Professor of Creative Writing at St. Lawrence University.

PAM HOUSTON has published two well-received books of short fiction, *Waltzing the Cat* and *Cowboys Are My Weakness.* Her well-reviewed collection of essays is called *A Little More About Me.* She teaches at the University of California, Davis.

FENTON JOHNSON is a regular contributor to *Harper's Magazine* and the author of two novels (*Crossing the River* and *Scissors, Paper, Rock*), a memoir (*Geography of the Heart: A Memoir*), and the forthcoming *Beyond Belief: A Skeptic's Journey Toward Faith*. He is on the faculty of the Creative Writing Program at the University of Arizona.

MAXINE KUMIN has published many books of poetry including *Our Ground Time Here Will Be Brief, The Long Approach, Nurture, Looking for Luck* and *Connecting the Dots*. Her recent memoir is *Inside the Halo and Beyond*. Ms. Kumin has written a mystery, *Quit Monks or Die!* among other books of fiction and many collections of essays, including *Always Beginning: Essays on a Life in Poetry*. This essay won the Ruth Lilly Award of the Modern Poetry Association in 1999.

DENISE LEVERTOV received the sixty-first Fellowship of the Academy of American Poets for distinguished poetry achievement. Before her death in December, 1997, she published numerous books of poems, essays, translations and memoirs. Her posthumous volume, *This Great Unknowing*, was published by New Directions in 1999.

DAVID MAS MASUMOTO has published books of short fiction, oral history and memoir. *Epitaph for a Peach* won the 1995 International Association of Culinary Professionals Award for best literary food writing. *Harvest Son*, published in 1998, won a Silver Medal Award in the 1999 California Books Awards by the Commonwealth Club and was a finalist in the 1999 Asian American Literary Awards. He writes often for *USA Today* and the *Los Angeles Times*. His "Sun Crest Peach" was included as part of the "Art of Taste" sponsored by the International Slow Food Movement.

WILLIAM MATTHEWS, the author of a dozen books of poetry, won the National Book Circle Award for *Time and Money* in 1995 and the Ruth Lilly Award of the Modern Poetry Association in 1997. He was born in Cincinnati and educated at Yale and the University of North Carolina. At the time of his death, he was a professor of English and director of the writing program at the College of the City University of New York. *After All: Last Poems* is now out in paperback.

LISA SHEA, author of *Hula*, has a new novel, *The Free World*, forthcoming from W.W. Norton, as well as a book of nonfiction. In 1999 she was the Tennessee Williams Fellow in Fiction at the University of the South at Sewanee, Tennessee. She has taught creative writing at Barnard College, Bennington College and the University of Massachusetts at Amherst. She lives in Brooklyn, New York, with her son Jonathon and their Yorkie, Scarlet.

JOAN WEIMER'S memoir *Back Talk: Teaching Lost Selves to Speak* was built entirely from her journal and has been adapted into a one-woman play that is performed around the U.S. She has coedited *Literature of America*, and she edited *Women Artists, Women Exiles*, a collection of stories by Constance Fenimore Woolson.

STEVEN WINN is the coauthor of a book on a serial killer, *Ted Bundy: The Killer Next Door*, and another on theater, *Great Performances: A Celebration*. His stories have appeared in *Good Housekeeping, Modern Maturity, Utne Reader, Parenting, The New York Times,* and *The Seattle Times* among other publications. He is the theater critic for the *San Francisco Chronicle*.

SHAWN WONG has written two novels, *American Knees* and *Homebase*. He won the Pacific Northwest Booksellers Award and the fifteenth Annual Governor's Writers Day Award of Washington. He is an editor and coeditor of many anthologies of Asian American Literature including *The Big Aiiieeeee! An Anthology of Chinese American and Japanese American Literature*. He has published poetry, essays and fiction in numerous literary magazines and has had his plays and screenplays produced. He co-wrote the screenplay for Celestial Pictures. He received the National Endowment for the Arts Creative Writing Fellowship and a Rockefeller Foundation residency in Italy. He was featured in the 1997 PBS documentary "Shattering the Silences." He is currently Chairman of the Department of English at the University of Washington.

AL YOUNG'S *Drowning in the Sea of Love* won the 1995 PEN/USA Award for the best nonfiction of the year. His work also includes the novels *Seduction by Light, Sitting Pretty, Who Is Angelina?* and the poetry collections *Heaven* and *Conjugal Visits*. He coauthored *Mingus Mingus: Two Memoirs* with Janet Coleman and wrote *Drowning in the Sea of Love: Musical Memoirs*. He has edited *African American Literature: A Brief Introduction and Anthology* and, along with Jack Hicks, James D. Houston and Maxine Hong Kinston, *The Literature of California*. His honors include the Wallace Stegner, Guggenheim, National Endowment for the Arts and Fulbright Fellowships as well as the PEN-Library of Congress Award for Short Fiction and the PEN-USA Award for Nonfiction. He has written scripts for Bill

Cosby and Richard Pryor and taught at Stanford University, the University of Michigan, the University of Washington, the University of California Berkeley, the University of California Santa Cruz, the University of Arkansas and Saint Mary's College among others.

INDEX